Her Voice | Her Story | Her Triumph

HER'D

ANTHOLOGIES

Sharria Crockett   Briana Nicole   Jacquia Paul   Ilene Fernandez

Yulonda Joy Beatty   Tonekia Williams   Dr. Unique C. Starks

Title: Her'D Anthologies: My Voice, My Story, My Triumph*

Authors: Tonekia Williams and Co-Authors

Cover Design: Masou B

Interior Design: Tonekia Williams

Edited by: Tonekia Williams

First Edition, 2025

Printed in the United States of America

This is a work of nonfiction. The stories shared in this anthology are based on true personal experiences. Some names and identifying details have been changed to protect privacy.

ACKNOWLEDGEMENTS

First and foremost, I give all glory and honor to God, who has been my source of strength, vision, and healing. Without His divine guidance, this book would not be possible.

I, Tonekia Williams, am deeply honored to stand beside six phenomenal women-Briana Nicole, Ilene Fernandez, Yulanda Joy Beatty, Dr. UniQue C. Starks, Sharria Crockett, and Jaquia Paul. Each of you brought truth, vulnerability, and strength to these pages. Thank you for trusting this vision and using your voice to inspire healing and hope.

To our families, friends, and loved ones-thank you for your patience, encouragement, and constant support as we poured our hearts into this work.

To every reader: may this book remind you that your voice matters, your story is sacred, and your triumph is possible. You are not alone. You are now apart of the family!

Chapter 1

A MOMENT AT THE WELL

Briana Nicole is a certified biblical life coach, heating advocate, and the CEO of Enamor Effect Through her coaching and resources, she helps women of faith heat from trauma, let go of emotional burdens, and embrace their God-given identity. Briana's journey of overcoming infertility, PCOS, domestic violence, and generational trauma has fueled her passion for guiding others toward wholeness.

Briana Nicole

She is the author of multiple self-guided healing resources and is passionate about merging faith with practical strategies for growth. As a storyteller and mentor, she creates spaces where women feel seen, empowered, and equipped lo walk in healing.

Her work has been featured on platforms that highlight faith, mental wellness, and personal transformation. Through her coaching programs and speaking engagements, Briana continues to inspire others to reclaim their power and step into the life God has called them to live.

A MOMENT AT THE WELL

He Loves Me... He Loves Me Not... He Loves Me!

That was one of my earliest memories—sitting in the front yard, plucking petals off daisies, hoping the last one would confirm that the boy I liked felt the same way. I was only five years old, yet I was already searching for validation. I didn't feel pretty. My chocolate skin, coarse hair, and full lips felt like flaws instead of features to be celebrated. But in my mind, if the right person liked me, then maybe—just maybe—I would be enough.

I didn't know it then, but I was already shaping my identity around how others saw me. That moment in the front yard was just a seed, planted deep, waiting to take root.

As I grew older, that need for acceptance didn't fade—it only intensified. By my teenage years, I wasn't just wondering if a boy liked me. I was questioning if I was enough for anyone. *Am I doing enough in this relationship? Am I worthy of this friendship? Do I belong?* My identity became woven into my connections with others. I wasn't just Briana—I was someone's girlfriend, someone's sister, someone's cousin, someone's friend. My worth wasn't something I could define on my own; it was something I borrowed from how others perceived me.

I see so much of myself in the story of the Woman at the Well. She, too, was nameless in her own story, known only by the men who had come and gone from her life. Her worth, in the eyes of her community, was reduced to her relationships—who she had been with, who she was connected to. And for so long, I lived the same way. I didn't recognize my own value outside of who I was to someone else.

But just like the Woman at the Well, I was on the brink of a moment that would change everything. A moment that would force me to face myself, to sit with my reflection, and to finally ask—*Who am I, outside of the people I've tried so hard to belong to?*

I always wondered how the Woman at the Well came to be. What was her story? Who was she outside of the five or six husbands she supposedly had? Was she anything like me? Was she really a villain, or was she just a woman searching for love?

Over the years, I've learned that we are all the villains in somebody's story. Maybe she felt she was simply surviving, making the best choices she could with what she had, while others saw her as a homewrecker or worse. What if she was just trying to meet some impossible societal standard, and her efforts were misunderstood?

I know what it's like to feel like no matter what you do, it's never enough.

From a young age, I noticed things that didn't sit right with me—things that made me feel different. My first experience with this was within my own family. My mom, my dad, and I all shared the same pecan tan complexion, but my younger sister? She was what we call in the South, *high yellow*—a stark contrast.

I was about three years old when my mom was pregnant with her, and I remember her telling me, *She's going to look just like you, and you're going to have to protect her.* In my little mind, that meant she would be mine—my baby, my twin.

But when she was born, she didn't look like me at all.

I made it my mission to protect her. But even as I took on the role of big sister, I couldn't ignore that things felt... different. She would hit me, and when I retaliated with my full strength, I got in trouble.

Don't hit her, you'll leave a bruise.

But if she hit me? Silence.

Looking back, I can't say for sure if my feelings of being treated differently were fully developed then, or if I simply understood that she was younger and naturally received more grace. But that seed was planted.

And then, we moved to Germany.

Both of my parents were in the military, so I was no stranger to relocation, but nothing could have prepared me for this. In Augusta, I was surrounded by kids who looked like me. In Germany, I was the only Black girl in my class, treated like an outsider simply because of the way I looked.

Even my teacher joined in.

I'll never forget Mr. Smith, my third-grade teacher, with his pale skin and red hair, standing at the front of the classroom as he read aloud our spelling words for the week.

"Weave—like how people make baskets... or like what Briana has in her hair."

SIR!!

At eight years old, I didn't know how to stand up for myself, especially against an adult. But one thing about it—I was not about to let those kids play in my face every day. If they had the nerve to come for me, they better have been ready for what came next.

Because one thing about growing up Black in the South? You don't come home if you lose a fight. You go back out there and handle it. So I fought—verbally, physically, however necessary.

I had to.

I didn't feel protected by the people who were supposed to protect me, so I learned to protect myself.

Right before fifth grade, we moved back to Augusta. Back to my old house, my old school, my old friends. And just like that, my aggression began to fade. I didn't have to fight to be seen.

But things had changed.

The culture had shifted.

When I was younger, I wanted to be just like Aaliyah and Monica—soft, stylish, effortlessly cool. But now? We were two years post-Tip Drill and right in the middle of the BET *Uncut* era. The beauty standard had changed. And I didn't fit.

I constantly heard rappers glorify light-skinned, curvy "redbones" while I stood on the sidelines—slim, dark-skinned, and rocking short hair. The message was loud and clear: girls who looked like me weren't the standard.

I felt like I had to overcompensate in every way. I couldn't be the prettiest, but I could be the smartest. I could be the most accomplished. I could prove that I was worthy.

But that feeling of not being enough followed me everywhere—from home, to school, to every relationship I ever found myself in. I felt like I had to earn my place.

At 11, I taught myself to play *If I Ain't Got You* by Alicia Keys—by ear. Excitedly, I ran to show my dad, expecting praise, acknowledgment, something.

Instead, he said,
"So when are you going to learn to sing and play at the same time?"

Maybe, in his mind, he was pushing me to be better. But in mine? I heard, *What you did wasn't enough.*

And that moment? That moment set the stage for everything that followed.

I became addicted to achievement.

If I wasn't pretty enough, if my talents weren't enough, then my accomplishments would be—because they were undeniable. I had proof.

I learned to measure my worth in trophies, certificates, and accolades. Success became my drug of choice.

At 10 years old, I broke down over a 92 because it meant I was no longer at the top of my class. I won the school spelling bee that year, but somehow, that still wasn't enough.

By high school, I had a 3.77 GPA—impressive by most standards. But at my magnet school, where excellence was expected, that GPA ranked me 40th out of 80. Once again, I felt invisible.

So I chased more.

I joined every honor society I could. I collected awards like armor, hoping they would shield me from the feeling of never being enough.

But even after college, even after graduating from the honors program, the emptiness remained. No matter how many achievements I stacked, I was still overlooked. Still unseen. Still searching for something—or someone—to finally convince me that I was enough.

To be honest, I think I may have even placed finding love above my accomplishments.

Why?

Because I knew myself—I knew that, no matter what, I would succeed academically. I always had. Somehow, I just figured it out. Love, on the other hand, wasn't that easy. Love was the one thing I had never truly experienced, and I craved it.

Growing up, love wasn't something that was spoken in our house.

My parents were both in the military—my mother, a drill sergeant who ran our household with precision, and my father, far more laid-back but still emotionally distant.

My sister and I were raised to be numb to everything. Vulnerability wasn't an option. Emotions weren't acknowledged.

The first hug I remember from my mom was at 18, right before I left for college. Compliments? Never heard them. Affirmation? Didn't exist.

The things that made me cry at night weren't up for discussion.

"You don't let anyone make you cry," was the standard response. And that was that.

So I searched for what I lacked in the men I dated.

I wanted someone I could dream with, someone I could be vulnerable with, because that was never allowed in my home.

But love quickly became a game of survival.

If I sensed a man pulling away, I had another lined up. I never let myself be alone because alone felt like rejection.

If one didn't work out, I already had a backup.

Even though I knew deep down my movements weren't healthy.

Every time something went left, it felt like another reminder that I wasn't enough.

Keeping my options open felt like protection—a safeguard against the pain of being unwanted.

By 16, my relationships had become a revolving door.

I had secretly been involved with practically an entire basketball team—not in a way that made me feel ashamed, but in a way that reflected just how desperately I wanted to be wanted.

It wasn't about sex.

It was about filling the void.

Each one validated me in a different way, but none of them could make me feel whole.

Then, I met my first love.

He changed everything—or so I thought.

We met on February 13, 2009, and by Valentine's Day, we were locked in.

I remember thinking he was completely out of my league—tall, light-skinned, green eyes, a football build, one of the most sought-after boys in his town.

There was no way he could have been interested in me.

But he was.

And for the first time, it wasn't about what I could offer physically—he didn't even know me like that yet.

Three months in, I was drowning in a kind of love I had never felt before. It was new. It was consuming. And I knew I never wanted it to end.

We survived a near-death experience within 2 weeks of each other, a trauma that bonded us even deeper.

Everything felt perfect.

Or so I thought.

The pressure I had felt to find love, to meet the expectation of marriage and motherhood, suddenly felt like it was becoming a reality.

I couldn't see myself with anyone else but him.

And even though we were long distance, I believed that wouldn't last for long. I had planned to go to college 30 minutes away from him. He was supposed to play football at UGA—every Georgia boy's dream—but he said he wanted to be near me.

At 16, I thought it was dumb but romantic.

At 32, I see it for what it was—a red flag.

Why would someone throw away their lifelong dream for a relationship that hadn't even reached its first anniversary?

Still, I was convinced he would be in my life forever.

We talked about getting married, having kids.

The pressure I once felt to find love was replaced with the comfort of believing I already had it.

Almost a year into the relationship, the whispers started.

People claimed he was cheating, but they had no proof—just speculation.

And I wasn't the type to act on rumors.

I needed facts.

Eventually, we broke up, and the truth behind it all surfaced later.

I bring up this relationship because it was my first real experience with love—at least, what I thought love was at the time.

It wasn't about sex.

It was about connection.

It was about finally feeling seen.

I never thought I could be loved like that.

And once I had that feeling, I never wanted to live without it.

Shortly after, I met someone new—for the sake of this story, let's call him David.

David checked every superficial box.

Athletic. Tattoos. Rough around the edges.

And did I mention he was fine?!

In high school, it felt lighthearted yet deeply emotional.

But this time, there were red flags—many of them.

David's emotions felt calculated.

He only showed vulnerability on Sundays, always followed by something physical.

My best friend and I even had a name for it—"Sentimental Sundays."

And then, there was his home life—volatile, chaotic, shaping him into someone who loved in a way that hurt.

Did I ignore all the signs?

Absolutely.

In the words of my grandmother, *"If it was a snake, it would've bit me."*

But I was too blinded by the love-bombing to see the venom.

He showered me with compliments, told me how much he wanted to be with me, and painted a picture of a future I so desperately wanted.

And I clung to it, even when reality showed me something different.

I kept having this recurring dream—one where we lived in a ranch-style house, a big black Tahoe parked in the yard.

The kitchen looked exactly like the one from my childhood home.

I was cooking, and he came in, wrapping his arms around me, kissing me on the cheek.

That dream kept me high on hope, making me laugh off the red flags I should have ran from.

Like the time he accused me of cheating—because I had a cold.

It was April, in Georgia, and my pollen allergies were in full force.

I explained it once, but he wouldn't hear it.

He was convinced there was someone else, and he spiraled.

Instead of taking it for what it was—irrational and toxic—I shrugged it off and kept moving.

Then came the night he called me frantic.

His father had waited until David left for the weekend to go out of town, then returned home and brutally beat his mother—cracking her ribs, breaking her wrist, and leaving her with a black eye.

My immediate reaction?

Protect David.

In my eyes, he was innocent.

He had witnessed so much violence from his father, and I convinced myself he would never be like him.

I was wrong.

The abuse started subtly, then escalated.

By the time I saw it for what it was, I was already in too deep.

I finally walked away.

But even after David, the pattern continued.

I chased love like a prize to be won, believing that if I could just find the right man, I would finally be enough.

And yet, time after time, I was left heartbroken. Embarrassed. Empty.

Because the real issue was never about finding love—it was about finding myself.

I didn't always make better choices in love because I felt like time was slipping away from me.

I had a checklist—get married, have kids, build a family—and I wanted to be done having children by the time I was 30.

That timeline dictated everything.

My standards were all over the place, shifting to fit whoever showed me interest.

I just wanted someone who genuinely loved me.

CHASING HEALING: FINDING WORTH AT THE WELL

I chased that feeling in all the wrong places. At 19, I dated a single father. Then a drug dealer. A childhood friend. Even a pastor who was a registered sex offender. After that, a mentally unstable veteran. It didn't make sense. Relationship after relationship, I ended up not just heartbroken but embarrassed. And that's what stung the most—not just the pain of the breakup, but the shame of realizing I had once again put my worth in the hands of someone who didn't deserve it.

Then, May 2018 happened.

My grandmother had just had a stroke, and I was experiencing the deepest heartbreak of my life up until that point. She could barely move, and somehow, neither could I. It felt like my heart had been ripped straight from my chest, leaving me paralyzed in a pain I never saw coming.

At 24 years old, I made a decision—I was done with pointless relationships. My next one was going to be my last because I was ready for marriage and a family. I was convinced that I had paid my dues in heartbreak. I had survived manipulation, abuse, infidelity, and disrespect. So when I met this man, before we even had our first real outing (because it definitely wasn't a date), I asked God to make him my husband. I just knew I didn't have another failed relationship left in me.

But God, in His infinite wisdom, had other plans.

A little over a year later, I was picking up the shattered pieces of yet another broken heart.

It was at that moment reality slapped me in the face: *"It can't be everybody else if my relationships keep ending like this."* At 25, I was still young, still learning, but one thing was clear—there was a pattern, and I needed to get to the root of it.

I confided in my mentor, spilling my pain, and she handed me a book: *Positioning Yourself to Be a Wife* by Shameika Dean. Early on, the book called for a purge, and let me tell you, that purge changed everything. I wasn't just dealing with heartbreak—I was trapped in a generational cycle of trauma.

I started to understand that love, as I had known it, was shaped long before I ever entered my first relationship. Both of my parents came from broken homes. My maternal grandparents divorced when my mom was around 12, and the dysfunction ran deep—infidelity, betrayal, and wounds that never fully healed.

On my dad's side, I never knew my grandmother because she passed away before I was born, and my grandfather was never in the picture.

My maternal grandmother played a huge role in raising my sister and me, but she carried her own painful story. She was the daughter of a woman who was what my family called "deaf and dumb." My great-grandmother, a stunning woman with deep, rich brown skin, had been married multiple times despite never being able to hear the words *"I love you."* And my grandmother—she was the product of rape. Raised by a woman who didn't birth her and never receiving a single *"I love you"* from her own mother, she went on to marry multiple times herself, always searching for something she never received.

On my father's side, his mother was technically married, but my grandfather abandoned her and their five children (later six) in South Carolina to start a new life in New York shortly after my father was born. He sent a measly $25 a month while he had other children with other women. My dad watched his mother struggle, vowing that when he made it, he'd take care of her. And he did—until the day she died.

I don't know what my parents' love looked like in the beginning, but by the time I came into the world on August 6, 1992, every ounce of their unhealed trauma was wrapped up in how they parented me.

And for years, I resented them for it.

It wasn't until May 2018 that I realized I had to give my parents grace. The expectations I had placed on them were unrealistic. I was demanding that they excel at something they had never been taught. Even when it came to my dreams and goals, I was doing something they had never done. I was the first person on my mother's side to go to college and actually graduate. So many before me had dropped out, struggling as single mothers. And somewhere along the way, I had absorbed the idea that having children young was a badge of honor—when in reality, so many of them were barely surviving.

That realization didn't erase my longing for children. If anything, it made it stronger.

Then, Valentine's Day 2021 happened.

That day, anxiety hit me like a tidal wave. It seemed like all the work I had been doing in therapy was undone. I was 28 years old. Not married. No kids. No house. I hadn't even bought a car before, yet somehow, I was supposed to be the "successful" one in my family. Everything I had expected to accomplish before 30 felt impossibly out of reach.

And in that moment—through my frustration, through my disappointment—God spoke: *The Enamor Effect.*

I had no clue what it meant. But He led me back to my psychology and social work studies—reminding me of the purpose I thought I had lost.

Years earlier, I had been on track to become a counselor, pursuing my master's at Florida A&M, when PCOS disrupted my plans. My health forced me to abandon that dream. And yet, here I was, being called back to it.

The deeper I dove into my work, the more I started to heal. I started to understand my pain—not as punishment, but as preparation.

God had never abandoned me.

I had been so consumed with trying to fit into my own expectations that I never stopped to ask if they were mine to carry. I had been so focused on being chosen that I never stopped to choose myself.

And for the first time, I realized—I didn't need a relationship to prove my worth. I didn't need a husband to validate me. I didn't need anyone's approval to know I was enough.

I always have been.

Growth found me, and then, so did my son.

Becoming a mother was a miracle in itself—one that not everyone celebrated. I was living life on my own terms, but that also came with judgment. My parents had waited until marriage to have children, and now here I was, a single mother. Some saw it as shameful. I saw it as divine.

Doctors had told me I would never conceive naturally, yet here I was, carrying life with no medical intervention. And the same doctor who once delivered my diagnosis now had to confirm what God had already spoken: my pregnancy was healthy.

Bringing my son into the world opened my eyes in ways I never expected. He was teaching me just as much as I was preparing to teach him. I knew what I didn't want him to believe about love. I didn't want him to grow up seeing a distorted version of it—one where his mother settled, where she clung to things that hurt her, where she was anything less than deeply loved. I wanted him to witness love in its healthiest form so that, one day, he would give that same love to whoever came into his life.

Motherhood also taught me about obedience. At the time, I was living in Tallahassee, Florida, but I was homesick. I started spending more and more time back in Augusta, staying for weeks at a time. In November, my elected lady asked me to join the women's retreat, saying it would be good for me to go before having the baby. I agreed, planning to return to Tallahassee afterward.

But when the retreat ended, something in my spirit told me: *Don't go back.*

So, I listened.

A week later, I had my 30-week appointment in Tallahassee. Instead of returning immediately, my sister drove me five and a half hours for the appointment, then drove us back to Augusta afterward. Two days later, I went into preterm labor.

Had I been in Tallahassee, I would have been completely alone, stuck in a hospital while my son spent six weeks in the NICU. But because I was in Augusta, I had my family, my church, and my son's father by my side. God had already positioned me where I needed to be.

For a while, I thought my son was the final piece of my healing. In my mind, his birth was confirmation that I had been made whole.

Back in 2016, when I was diagnosed with PCOS, my world shattered. I had just experienced deep betrayal from people I considered immediate family, and in the middle of that pain, I was told I might never have children. My body was reacting to my environment, warning me that I was carrying too much—mentally, emotionally, spiritually.

But healing my body wasn't about medicine. It was about release.

The moment I let go of those people, my body healed itself. Within a month of disconnecting from them for good, I conceived my son naturally. I thought that was the lesson—that I had been freed from everything that once plagued me.

And then, February 29, 2024, happened.

A month before, I found out I was pregnant again. This time, something felt different. I was extremely sick. I was bigger than expected. Could this have been the little girl I had always wanted? As the first trimester ended, my symptoms faded, but I still hadn't had my first appointment.

Then, the unthinkable happened—no heartbeat.

I couldn't contain myself. While I wasn't actively planning for another child, I knew that if I had one, we would be okay. But now, I had to carry the weight of losing a child and the fear of disappointing my parents all over again. I was the "mess up" again.

So, I did what I had always done—I moved through it in silence.

On the day of my procedure, I dropped my son off at daycare. My son's father and I went to the hospital. I had the D&C, and we returned home in time to pick up our son. Just like that, we had to act as if nothing had happened.

Then, before I could even begin to process my grief, my aunt and uncle passed away within days of each other.

I was furious. Furious at life. Furious at God. Furious that I had given Him everything and still, He had taken my baby. I couldn't make sense of it. I wrestled with the questions that clawed at my soul: *Why would You take an innocent baby? What did I do to deserve this? How can You say You make no mistakes, yet allow this to happen?*

For months, I was drowning in grief. I wanted to throw God away completely. But healing doesn't happen without confrontation. And I had to confront God. I questioned Him. I screamed. I cried. I wrestled with my faith in a way I never had before.

And after seven months of silence, I finally got my answer.

My baby was due the same day Hurricane Helene hit Augusta.

Of course, I didn't understand it at the time. But when the storm came, and the city shut down for weeks, I realized—He was protecting us. I couldn't see it then, but God was never punishing me. He was preserving me.

That realization forced me to return to my faith.

For the first time, I had to be honest with myself. I had expected God to reward me for my healing—as if I were now exempt from pain. I had felt entitled, believing that after everything I had endured, nothing like this would ever happen to me.

But healing doesn't mean life won't hurt you again. It doesn't mean you'll never be tested.

Healing is a lifelong journey. And it is always worth the fight.

Here I was... at my well.

I had spent years drawing from empty places, hoping to fill myself with something that could never satisfy me. I had searched for validation in the eyes of men, in achievements, in relationships that left me drained and hollow. I thought love was something I had to earn, something I had to chase. But just like the Woman at the Well, I found myself face to face with the truth—I was never meant to be defined by who I was connected to. My worth had been there all along.

The Woman at the Well came seeking water, but what she found was something far greater—freedom. She left that well transformed, no longer bound by the opinions of others, no longer defined by her past.

And like her, I am no longer waiting for someone else to tell me who I am. I am no longer looking to be chosen.

I choose me.

And that is what healing is—choosing yourself, every single day. It's unlearning the lies that told you that you weren't enough. It's breaking the cycle of seeking approval from people who were never meant to give it to you. It's standing in the fullness of who you are and knowing that you are already worthy, already loved, already whole.

So if you are at your well, searching for something to make you feel like you are enough—stop looking outward. The love, the validation, the healing you are searching for has been within you all along. You just have to choose it.

And when you do, you'll never thirst again.

Chapter 2

HOW DO YOU LET GO OF SOMETHING THAT BECAME A PART OF YOU?

The world I once knew was shattered

Ilene Fernandez, born and raised in Brooklyn, NY, is a proud mother of three and holds degrees in Psychology. She is the author of Oh NO! Where Did the Baby Go? and Bri Wonders Why?, and co-author of From Hurting to Healing.

Ilene is the founder of KDA Foundation Inc., established in honor of her late fiance. As a Behavior Analyst with over a decade of experience in the NYC Department of Education, she supports children with autism through positive behavior strategies and skill-building.

ILENE FERNANDEZ

Her writing is a vital part of her healing journey, offering inspiration and connection through hope and shared experience.

Follow her on Instagram: .@kda foundation inc and TikTok: @kda foundation inc

HOW DO YOU LET GO OF SOMETHING THAT BECAME A PART OF YOU?

The world I once knew was shattered.

LOVE—how do we define it?
Love looks, feels, and shows up differently for everyone.

What's your love language?
Mine is food, snacks, TV shows, music, and a good ole foot rub.

"Love met me when" I felt peace, free, and like a kid again. When I felt like I was the only woman that existed in the world.

Let me tell you about my love story.

Someone once asked me, "How would you define your love?" I responded:

Like Martin and Gina (TV show). A best friend, someone I could talk to about my doubts, fears, and worries. My happiness, joy, and precious moments. A shoulder to lean on. My confidant.

My love felt magical and was built on a friendship.

Life has a way of genuinely surprising you. Who would've known that the boy I used to hang around with through mutual friends—the one whose house I chilled at around age 10 but barely spoke to—the one I'd walk past and who'd make me laugh with his salty facial expression, would become my everything?

My best friend.
My authentic love.

The father of my children.

My fiancé.

I wouldn't have wanted it any other way.

Kevin had always been a ball of fun. As soon as I saw him, I'd laugh—knowing something wild was about to come out of his mouth. He had a smooth charm that could turn any mundane moment into something hilarious. Kevin saw the world through the lens of humor. He'd crack jokes at the most random and inappropriate moments. His ability to lighten up any room was unreal. That smile of his—that was his trademark.

We had a few years between us. Those years for me were filled with both joy and challenges—one joy being the birth of my first-born son.

Kevin and I reunited in our early twenties at a backyard BBQ. Fate said it was time for us to reconnect. That familiar smile was still there. From that moment, we began building a life together. Before dating, we had a real friendship.

I remember telling one of my friends, "He's such a good guy. I hope he finds a great woman." Little did I know, that woman would be me.

Music became the soundtrack to our relationship. Our car rides were therapeutic karaoke sessions. We'd send each other songs over text or hum them over the phone, trying to guess the artist and lyrics. This became our thing. But it wasn't just about music—it was how those songs expressed what we felt about each other. R&B became our secret language.

There were times I feared if I had made the right decision leaving the father of my son. Kevin always reassured me. And in those reassurances, I knew I'd made the right choice. He made me laugh. Our deep conversations brought us even closer. When we talked, the outside world disappeared. I felt seen, heard, and understood.

Kevin brought more than laughter—he brought support. Especially with my dreams. The most powerful part was how he stepped into the father role for my son, Akeel, who was only three when Kevin re-entered my life. Kevin loved him like his own.

He was there for school shows, taught him how to ride a bike, tie his shoes, and always emphasized respect. Kevin built up his confidence and protected it like a shield. He'd help with homework, bathe him, and make sure he was set for the next school day. That wasn't just love—that was fatherhood. I respected and admired him deeply for that.

Kevin believed in us.

Our foundation was love, support, and commitment. We were building a future together, brick by brick. He celebrated all my wins, big or small. He was my biggest cheerleader.

Our first movie date was at Court Street Theater—we saw The Town. I felt butterflies. Sitting next to him in that dark theater, it wasn't just the film that felt important—it was him.

He helped me discover things about myself I didn't know existed. In his eyes, I was enough. And through his love, I started to believe it too.

At the time, I lived in Queens, but worked and had Akeel in school in Brooklyn. I started staying at Kevin's during the week. He'd drop Akeel off and take me to work before starting his own day. If he could, he'd bring me lunch and we'd sit in the car talking through my break.

He'd joke, "I let you spend a night once and you never left."

Kevin loved simplicity. For his birthday, all he wanted was a slice of Junior's chocolate cake. But I made sure he felt celebrated. Every year on my birthday, he turned into a whole light show—waking me at midnight, singing some ridiculous yet sweet song. That wide grin, those goofy lyrics—unforgettable.

One of our relationship's theme songs was "Something in Common" by Whitney Houston and Bobby Brown. That was us—two people transforming, growing together.

In 2014, we reached a new chapter. We moved into our first apartment in Brooklyn and welcomed our baby boy, Carter— Kevin's first biological child. Watching him father both boys was beautiful. He was nurturing, patient, and protective.

Even though Kevin valued sleep, he'd wake up at night with Carter so I could rest. He sacrificed without complaint.

He made time for the boys—parks, life lessons, memories.

Sundays were our family day. We would enjoy games, laughter and facials. I usually gave Kevin his facial after he watched his sports and my Sunday dinner was complete. Once the boys were in bed. It was time for us, our couch and shows. We would take turns rubbing each other's heads. Kevin would joke, "I don't know about you, but I'm going in the room," and of course I'd follow.

Most nights, I'd fall asleep to him massaging my feet while watching TV.

Coming home from work, he'd have my favorite snacks and a vanilla milkshake waiting. Store-bought or homemade. He always knew how to bring me peace.

He'd say, "You know I love you, boo," with that playful tone.

On my birthday—June 23, 2021—Kevin proposed in the most magical way. It was creative, real, and perfect. All the laughter, struggles, and quiet moments led to that. It felt like just the beginning.

We dreamed of a wedding, blending our visions. Kevin wanted a baby girl—after a miscarriage, I found out in August 2021, I was pregnant again. When we learned it was a girl, he was overjoyed. He wanted her name to start with "B" and called our kids his "alphabets."

We laughed and joked about them being out of order. Every visit, Kevin was there, cracking jokes and calling her his princess. He watched over everything I ate and made sure I was okay. Kevin stepped up at home, grocery shopping, laundry and anything else I needed.

He even drove me to work and took the boys to school on his days off. Never once complaining of his lack of sleep.

During rides, I'd sing, "I love you just because…" and he'd laugh, "You always wanna play," then start singing "Just because I do…"

Then he'd turn on Anita Baker. That music was us.

But life has a way of surprising you. This time, it was cruel.

On a regular day, I was woken from sleep. Kevin's sister told me he'd been rushed to the hospital.

I was confused and in total shock—we had just talked. I was two weeks from delivering our baby girl.

This couldn't be happening. Not Kevin.

I called everyone, crying and screaming. Most didn't believe me or were just as numb.

I took an Uber to the hospital, so many family and friends were already there. The fear was overwhelming.

Everything was a blur. My thoughts ran wild. I prayed hard, hoping it wasn't as serious as it seemed.

But then came the call—from the neurosurgeon. Kevin's condition was critical. I had to get to the hospital now.

I wasn't ready.

My love, my life, my partner...was gone.

I've felt pain. Deep pain. And every year, the pain remains.

But God—He continues to carry me.

There were days I stumbled, but I kept going.

This journey isn't about forgetting the pain. It's about learning to live with it. About rising, even when it hurts.

Each step forward is a testament to love. To Kevin. To grace. To purpose.

I hope you enjoyed the prelude to my love story. Stay tuned for my upcoming memoir;

Robbed of a Brooklyn Love Story.

Chapter 3

LUPUS TO LEMONADE

Diagnosed with Lupus at 13, Yulonda Joy Beatty's extraordinary journey is a testament to resilience and purpose. Facing significant health battles, she discovered strength and hope through her unwavering faith, deeply inspired by Romans 5:3-5--knowing that "perseverance shapes character and character fosters hope."

Drawing strength from these very experiences, Yulonda built her education and career with the same determination. Yulonda holds a BA in Psychology from Hampton University and an MBA from Howard University. As the founder and CEO of Integrity Matters Virtual

YULONDA JOY BEATTY

Solutions, LLC, she provides impactful office management and digital design services to life coaches and consultants. Passionate about encouraging others, she openly shares her testimony and is launching a faith-based podcast aimed at uplifting and empowering the Lupus community.

Driven by creativity, she also enjoys jewelry making, fashion design, and serving women and children in shelters, embodying her belief that life's lemons truly can be transformed into lemonade.

LUPUS TO LEMONADE

INTRODUCTION:
TURNING PAIN INTO PURPOSE

Romans 8:28 – "And we know that in all things God works for the good of those who love him, who have been called according to his purpose."

Sis, when life handed me Lupus at thirteen, I couldn't see beyond the pain. But over time, every struggle revealed a deeper faith and a greater purpose. The bitterness of Lupus didn't define my story—it transformed it. What started as sour lemons became a rich testimony of healing, joy, and resilience. This is my story of hope, strength, and the incredible power of trusting God through adversity.

Though my journey centers around Lupus, this message is for any woman walking through difficulty—whether it's illness, loss, heartbreak, or hardship. If life has handed you something heavy, I want you to know beauty is still ahead. God specializes in turning pain into purpose, regardless of its form. Your pain doesn't cancel your promise.

To the Newly Diagnosed: First Steps of Faith

Psalm 91:11 – "For he will command his angels concerning you to guard you in all your ways."

At thirteen, an ordinary afternoon turned frightening. I came home feeling short of breath and my heart racing. When I collapsed onto my mom's bed, we knew something was seriously wrong. I was rushed to the hospital, and after a whirlwind of tests and anxious waiting, the doctors finally returned with the results: pneumonia, heart inflammation, and something we had never heard before—Lupus.

They explained that Lupus is a chronic autoimmune disease where the body's immune system turns on itself, attacking healthy tissues and organs. It can affect the joints, skin, heart, lungs—basically, the whole body. I remember sitting there, overwhelmed and confused, trying to process words I didn't even understand.

Fear swept in, but my mom squeezed my hand and said, "God is going to take care of you." Even though I knew she was scared too, her faith helped settle mine. As I drifted in and out of sleep, I saw glowing white figures—women in white robes surrounding my bed. I woke up thinking they were nurses. When I asked my mom about them, she said, "Baby, those weren't nurses. Those were angels."

That hospital bed became holy ground. I didn't understand the path ahead, but faith began there. God was already laying the foundation for the strength I'd need.

Sis, if you're facing a battle without a support system, know this: God Himself will stand in the gap. When no one else knows how to show up for you, He will send a word, a stranger, or even an angel to remind you that you're not forgotten. You are seen, Sis. You are held.

To the Young and Insecure: Finding Identity Through the Fire

Psalm 139:14 – "I praise you because I am fearfully and wonderfully made; your works are wonderful, I know that full well."

At fifteen, Lupus flared up again—this time attacking my joints and lungs, walking to the school bus left me short of breath. I was diagnosed with Juvenile Rheumatoid Arthritis, which brought stiff, swollen, achy, and painful joints. My whole body hurt. My medications caused nausea, weight gain, and left me with a puffy face. I was teased with names like "Chubby Cheeks" and "Chipmunk." I laughed on the outside, but the words wounded me on the inside. Insecurity crept in, and I couldn't see myself beyond the illness.

Then I began reading the Word. Scriptures like 1 Peter 2:9 reminded me that I was chosen, loved, and set apart. Slowly, I began to see myself through God's eyes.

Healing wasn't linear. Even after embracing my identity in Christ, depression kept knocking. But those dark seasons taught me to lean into God's truth. My pain wasn't punishment—it was refining. Like lemonade, my life needed the sweetness of His promises to balance the bitterness.

Sis, comparison is a thief. When I stopped seeking confirmation from others and looked to God, I found peace. I started speaking kindly to myself and embracing the beauty of who I was becoming, not in spite of the scars, but because of them.

There's a version of you that exists on the other side of insecurity—bold, secure, and at peace with your reflection. Trust that she's in there, even when the mirror tries to lie.

I wasn't less than—I was being shaped for something greater.

Later, in my twenties, I had to undergo major neck surgery. The bone connecting my head to my spinal cord had deteriorated from arthritis. I wore a halo vest—bolts drilled into my skull to stabilize my spine. I couldn't move freely or lie flat. Even bathing required assistance. It was one of the most vulnerable seasons of my life. I remember telling my doctor that I wanted to take pills so I wouldn't have to wake up. I was emotionally exhausted, physically restricted, and spiritually worn thin.

I was hospitalized for psychiatric care, not because I lacked faith, but because I needed help. And God met me there.

Through therapy, time, and grace, I rose. Healing looked like stillness, tears, and trust. The halo-vest, the hospital bed, the tear-stained pillow—they became altars where I surrendered the image of strength and let God restore my worth.

If you're in the fire right now, Sis, don't be afraid.

God is refining you, not rejecting you. You are still His masterpiece.

To the Long-Suffering: Endurance for the Marathon

Romans 5:3-5 – "Not only so, but we also glory in our sufferings, because we know that suffering produces perseverance; perseverance, character; and character, hope."

After high school, Lupus eased just enough for me to chase my dreams. I graduated from Hampton University in 1992 and earned my MBA from Howard in 2000. I bought a home in Laurel, Maryland, and started working at a neonatal healthcare practice. Life felt full until Lupus came roaring back, this time attacking my kidneys. I was diagnosed with renal failure and told I needed dialysis. I left my job, home, and independence behind, and moved to Augusta to live with my mom. Everything I had worked for felt snatched away.

Even with my mom's support, I felt alone. Now in my 30s, dialysis became my new rhythm—three days a week, four hours a session. I was tired, grieving, and searching for purpose. I clung to Jeremiah 29:11: "For I know the plans I have for you," declares the Lord. "Plans to prosper you and not to harm you, plans to give you hope and a future." God wasn't promising that everything would be easy, but He kept reassuring me to trust Him. His plans were still good.

One day, I brought my bead box to treatment and started making jewelry. What began as a distraction became a creative ministry— Everlasting Joy, my handmade jewelry business. Nurses, doctors, even patients began buying my pieces. Each bracelet was a drop of lemonade, made from pain and prayer. God used creativity to restore my confidence and give me purpose again.

Doctors said a kidney could take 3–5 years. By year five, another blow came. I contracted MRSA, and the infection destroyed my left hip. During surgery to remove the infected joint, the surgeon accidentally nicked an artery. I lost seven pints of blood and coded blue. The memory is still a blur. After weeks in the ICU, I had a hip replacement. I spent six months in the hospital and six more in rehab learning how to walk again, all while still on dialysis.

It was another season of deep suffering. I felt discouraged. But in year seven, I got the call, "We have a kidney for you." My transplant was at 7 a.m. on the 7th floor. God's number of completion showed up right on time. The healing wasn't just physical, it was spiritual.

Those seven years were more than waiting; they shaped me for purpose.

There were moments I questioned everything, but each setback was sacred soil. Like lemons pressed hard for juice, my faith was being squeezed, refined, and poured out.

Sis, if you're feeling weary, remember: "The race is not given to the swift, nor the battle to the strong, but to the one who endures to the end" (Ecclesiastes 9:11). This journey isn't a sprint—it's a marathon. Every step you take, no matter how slow, is still progress. Endurance isn't about speed—it's about not quitting. Keep going—your finish line holds more glory than you can imagine.

To the Caregiver: Honoring Those Who Serve

Galatians 6:2 – "Carry each other's burdens, and in this way, you will fulfill the law of Christ."

Throughout my journey, my mom was my constant. She showed up for every appointment, surgery, and sleepless night. Her presence gave me strength when mine gave out, and her words lifted me when hope wavered. I know it wasn't easy watching me suffer in pain, but she never let go of faith. God used her as His hands on earth. Her quiet love was ministry in motion. She was the sugar in my lemonade—stirring hope into bitter days.

I thank God for my mom every single day. Her love is one of the greatest gifts He's ever given me.

To every caregiver, you matter more than you know. You are the unseen heroes. The ones who pour out love, even when you're running on empty. God sees every act of kindness, every sacrifice. You are part of the miracle.

And if you're weary, please rest in this truth: you are not expected to carry the weight alone. God carries you as you carry others. You are not forgotten in your giving. You are covered in grace.

You may not wear a cape, but your quiet service is sacred. Your love speaks louder than any medicine, and your presence is often the healing someone else is praying for. You are light in hospital rooms, peace in chaotic moments, and strength in times of weakness. Your reward may not come as an applause, but trust me, it is recorded in heaven. Keep showing up. Your love is changing lives.

To the Woman Seeking Guidance: Recognizing Divine Direction

Luke 4:10 – "For it is written: 'He will command his angels concerning you to guard you carefully.'"

I know what it feels like to walk by faith when your body is failing and your future uncertain. Lupus isn't predictable. Five years after my transplant, everything was going well. In 2021, I started a Virtual Office Management business, Integrity Matters Virtual Solutions. I thought I was in the clear, but Lupus showed up again, this time in my spine. Nerve pain stole my sleep and strength.

In 2025, when doctors told me I needed spinal surgery, I didn't just seek medical advice. I sought God. I prayed, fasted, cried, and listened. People told me not to do it, but the Holy Spirit whispered, "Have the surgery—I've already made the way."

And He did. The surgery was a success. Healing came gradually, but God was in every detail. That chapter taught me that divine direction doesn't always shout; sometimes it whispers. Trust that voice.

Even when life squeezes, God is mixing something sweet. Let His Word and presence guide you. Stir your lemons with praise and pour them into purpose. When you're unsure, listen in closely. God's guidance may not come with flashing signs, but it always comes with peace.

Discernment isn't about knowing everything—it's about trusting the Holy Spirit enough to move, even in the unknown. Peace doesn't always lead the way; sometimes it meets you in motion. Every divine detour holds purpose, so don't fear the fog—if God called you, He will guide you.

TO FUTURE GENERATIONS: THE LEGACY OF FAITH

2 Corinthians 1:3-4 – "Praise be to the God...who comforts us in all our troubles, so that we can comfort those in any trouble with the comfort we ourselves receive from God."

My story isn't just about surviving Lupus—it's about purpose born through pain. God turned each sour season into something that could serve others.

For future generations, I want the legacy of my journey to be a testimony that empowers women. I want them to see that our deepest struggles, like my long battle with Lupus, can become the foundation for our greatest purpose. I hope they recognize that even when life hands you something unexpected, it doesn't have to define you. Instead, it can be transformed into something beautiful that blesses others.

I want to be remembered not for the pain I endured, but for how that pain was repurposed into something meaningful. My "Lupus to Lemonade" experience is more than a personal story; it's a roadmap. I hope women see themselves in these pages and realize that hardship doesn't diminish their value. In fact, challenges can awaken hidden strength, unlock creativity, and uncover divine purpose.

To the women who read this, I pray you:

Embrace your identity beyond any diagnosis or challenge.

Find healing in community.

Recognize the spiritual side of recovery.

See entrepreneurship as a calling, not just a career.

Your story, surrendered to God, becomes a survival guide for someone else. Your lemons can leave a legacy. Your life can refresh others.

And if you're holding your lemons, unsure of what to do with them, trust the process. The squeezing, the stirring, and the waiting are all part of the recipe. You are being prepared for something greater.

You are someone's answered prayer in the making. And one day, they'll thank God you didn't give up.

Conclusion: From Pain to Praise

Isaiah 61:3 – "...to bestow on them a crown of beauty instead of ashes, the oil of joy instead of mourning, and a garment of praise instead of a spirit of despair."

Turning pain into praise is sacred. Every tear you've cried has watered your growth. Every hardship has shaped, not shattered, you.

Sis, your scars aren't signs of defeat. They're evidence of endurance. Own them. Honor them. Let them fuel your future.

If you're in a lemon season, hold on. God's not finished. Your scars will become signs of grace. Your story will become someone else's survival guide.

The sleepless nights? They were lemons turned into prayer. The side effects and setbacks? Lemons crushed into compassion. The loss of independence? A lemon God used to stir up a new identity rooted in Him. And the closed doors? Lemons rerouted to divine appointments you couldn't have planned.

Sis, every sour thing you've endured is being stirred into something that will nourish others. This is your pitcher of praise. Keep pouring.

And that, my love, is the sweetest legacy of all.

Chapter 4

A UNIQUE LIFEE: FAITH, MOTHERHOOD, AND THE JOURNEY TO PURPOSE

Peace and Human Justice,

I am no longer accepting the things I cannot change. 1 am changing the things I cannot accept." -Angela Davis

Dr. UniQue C. Starks

Dr. UniQue C. Starks is a transformative organizer, social worker, and justice advocate committed to restoring and transforming communities and individuals across the African diaspora. Holding a Doctorate in Social Work (DSW) from the University of Southern California (USC) and a Master of Social Work (MSW) from New York University's Silver School of Social Work, Dr. Starks has organized and sustained over 1,000 global initiatives, emphasizing the power of partnerships and relationship building to drive change in restorative justice, mental health, and community empowerment.

As Director of Community Restorative Justice Initiatives at the Kings County DA's Office, she focuses on capacity building and accountability through a restorative and healing-centered approaches and works with diverse stakeholders to implement sustainable programs. Dr. Starks is also an adjunct professor at NYU, where she mentors and empowers future social justice leaders. She founded A UniQue Ufee, a social club for Black women in social justice, providing spaces for healing, resilience, and transformation.

A UNIQUE LIFEE: FAITH, MOTHERHOOD, AND THE JOURNEY TO PURPOSE

"The steps of a good man are ordered by the Lord, and He delights in his way." (Psalm 37:23)

I became a mother on August 4, 2012—the same birthday as President Barack Obama. That felt like a sign, a promise. My son, Anthony Jr. (AJ), arrived five weeks early but weighed in at 8 pounds, 11 ounces. From the very beginning, he carried both the weight of his own strength and the dreams I hadn't even formed yet. He was a blessing the moment I heard his heartbeat in my stomach in November 2011.

At 19, I was still a teenager, unsure of what success really looked like in 2012. I was definitely optimistic about the responsibilities of parenthood—maybe even naïve. But one thing I knew for sure: I would give my child the best of me. I made that promise the day I heard his heartbeat, and it deepened the moment he was born. We would do this life-thing together, and I would love AJ unconditionally.

It wasn't easy. AJ had anywhere from two to eight doctor's appointments every month until he was 8 years old. His health impacted my ability to work full-time and affected how I showed up in every area of my life. But my son was always my first priority. His first major surgery came when he was just 12 months old in 2013, to help his stomach digest food properly. Our life quickly became a cycle of hospital rooms, prayer circles, and long nights—holding my child in one arm and my faith in the other. Faith and fear can't exist in the same space. Still, I never felt alone. My tribe—friends, family, even medical staff—surrounded us with support. AJ's medical team gave us excellent care and constant reassurance. It was divine. God was showing up before I even knew how to name it.

My mother and late sister were ambivalent about me becoming a parent. They weren't sure what our life would look like or if I'd accomplish everything I said I would. I think they were scared. I think they doubted. And I get it—I was young. But what they didn't know then—and what I know now—is that I was being shaped for something much bigger than I could have imagined.

In 2017, I found God in an intimate, undeniable way.

AJ was five and preparing for eye surgery after specialists at New York Eye and Ear told us he was going blind and could potentially lose his vision completely by the time he turned 18. He was diagnosed with a rare condition, and my family already had a history of poor vision. But this time felt different. AJ was older, more aware. He had questions: "Why me?" "Why do I need surgery?" I didn't have the answers. But I held him and said, *"We'll go through this together"—*and I meant it. My mom and Big Anthony didn't leave our side for a second. They love AJ and me so deeply, and they were feeling the same pain.

Before the IV, AJ was given "funny gas," which made him hyper and anxious. He became aggressive, and I could feel my own anxiety rising. When they wheeled him away, I broke. I cried. I prayed. I begged God to cover him. When he came out—his eyes bloodied, crying, and confused—I had never felt more helpless in my life. That night, while he rested beside me, I picked up my Bible for the first time in years.

I had grown up in the Black church. My grandmother, a Protestant Christian, took me every week with my older cousins and baby cousin. To this day, I still wear dresses and skirts because of her teachings and the traditions of the Black church. I loved church—the Word, the music, the community, the feeling of belonging. "Sunday's best." The way Black folks showed up on Sundays in faith and fashion. But when my grandmother got sick, I drifted. Life got heavy, and church got hard. But in that hospital room, I felt God tap me on the shoulder and whisper, I'm with you.

My family started going to church together. We enrolled AJ in a Christian school. We began praying every day—in gratitude, before meals, and honestly, just because. When life didn't make sense, we knew we could still count on God. I began to realize: God wasn't just in the church. God was in our home, our offices, our conversations, the waiting rooms, the exam tables, the laughter between us in the car, the resilience in AJ's little body, and the strength I didn't know I had.

There's something powerful about community—especially when we come together in prayer. Matthew 18:20 reminds us that when two or three gather in God's name, He is right there with us the whole way. I've lived that truth over and over again. Whether in hospital waiting rooms, classrooms, or my living room surrounded by loved ones, I've felt God's presence show up through prayer. I've seen miracles I can't even explain. My tribe has never let me stand alone. When I was weak, they prayed. When I couldn't find the words, they prayed louder. That's what sustained me and helped me thrive.

On this journey, I've learned that faith doesn't always look the way we'd like. It's about trusting that things will unfold in their own time. AJ's healing journey wasn't the story I envisioned—his vision didn't reach the 20/20 I prayed for, but he is healthy, thriving, and full of life. I couldn't ask for more. What matters most is that he's here, surrounded by love, and that is more than enough.

Around the same time, I was finishing my master's degree at NYU's Silver School of Social Work. I already had two degrees, and by 2018, I had accomplished so much. I had kept the promises I made to myself and my family—but something still didn't feel right. I was successful in some ways, yes, but I was always on edge. That night in the hospital, something shifted. I realized: God doesn't want my perfection. God wants my presence. My partnership. My obedience.

From that day forward, I made another promise: I would center myself in God's will. I would follow God's footsteps.

Since then, I've earned a doctorate. I've built community programs rooted in humanity, justice, healing, and love. I've led teams. I've mentored others across the world. I've fought to dismantle systems that harm our people—and helped build new ones that transform, restore, and affirm. But above all, I've lived in relationship: as a mother, a partner, a daughter, a sister, an aunt, a friend—and most importantly, a believer and servant.

This journey has helped me discover my true passion and purpose. It shaped my desire to serve and uplift others. Through the challenges and the triumphs, I've learned that my calling lies in showing up, building, healing, and creating spaces for justice and community. It has grounded me in the understanding that my work is not just a profession—it's a mission to make the world better for those who need it most.

None of this would have been possible without God. Every door that opened, every room I stepped into, every hospital bed I sat beside, every class I completed, every courtroom I walked into—it's all because of Him. I don't always get it right. I'm human. But my intention is always love, always justice, and always rooted in faith and humility.

I see God in everyone I encounter. I see God in the systems I aim to transform. I see God in the community. I love my community. And I see God in my son's eyes—those same eyes I once prayed over, now wide open and full of life.

Chapter 5

THERE IS PURPOSE IN PAIN

Sharria Laverne Crockett was born and raised on the South Side of Chicago, Illinois. She is the youngest of four children and credits her grandmother and mother as the greatest influences in her life. Their strength, love, and guidance continue to shape the woman she is today.

Sharria is a proud mother to one son, whom she loves and cherishes with all her heart. She is a woman of God, an educator, author, mentor, and above all, a generational curse breaker. With a powerful passion for uplifting and restoring today's youth, she walks boldly in her God-given purpose.

Sllarria Crockett

As she continues to cultivate her life and grow in purpose, Sharria is committed to bringing others along on the journey-empowering like-minded individuals to pursue success not only financially, but also mentally, emotionally, and spiritually.

THERE IS PURPOSE IN PAIN

I'm just a young and vibrant girl from the South Side of Chicago, born and raised in the '90s where the vibes were always a good time. I'm the youngest of four children—very spoiled and usually used to getting my way. If you're the baby of the family, you know exactly what I mean. Because of that, my family has always been—and still is—super overprotective of me. Growing up around mostly boys—my older brother and a bunch of boy cousins—was a lot! I was scared to get a boyfriend because I knew they would probably run him off.

Growing up in a two-parent household with my siblings was beautiful. I love my family, and I value structure in the home. Now, I'm not saying everything was perfect, but I appreciated having both my parents raise us together. I believe that's why I'm so family-oriented today. I saw marriage first hand—not just with my parents, but also with both of my grandmothers, who stayed married to my grandfathers. One word: loyalty. I saw it, I witnessed it, I embody it, and I'm big on it.

My parents were a whole vibe growing up. I remember the sacrifices they made to keep our home in order and make sure we were taken care of. We had a ball—it was truly a good time. Summer nights were filled with laughter, watching my aunties and mama vibing on the porch, my grandma sitting at the front door, cousins, my brother, and neighbors all outside playing Red Light, Green Light. And the best part? Both of my grandparents lived on the same block—so it was always a good time.

I was raised in a Christian household, and my grandmother on my dad's side started taking me to children's church regularly at age seven. So, I always had a solid foundation. But I didn't truly understand the importance of building a relationship with God until I was sixteen. Let me tell you—when you're a chosen vessel, the enemy knows it. After I got baptized at sixteen, that's when I feel like the attacks on my adolescence really began.

Like most teenage girls, I hung out, drank alcohol, tried smoking, and liked boys. It's natural to want to feel loved, especially when you grew up witnessing real love at home. So yeah, I did the girlfriend thing—it was cool and cute... until I realized I didn't know my worth and kept settling.

I'm not here to bash anyone. That's not the point. The truth is, we can get so wrapped up in the idea of being with someone and wanting love, that we end up investing our time, bodies, and souls in the wrong relationships. I didn't just grow up with my mom—I grew up around loyal women like both of my grandmothers. That loyalty was ingrained in me. Even in friendships, I don't play about loyalty. If I love you, I'm ten toes down—right or wrong.

My first real relationship started at seventeen. I was young, I know, but for many, those last couple of years in high school are when relationships feel real. We had good times and bad times, and times when I knew I should've walked away. But the loyalty in me kept me locked in. Once I commit, I commit hard.

Even though I grew up in a Christian home, nobody ever explained soul ties to me, or the difference between godly and ungodly connections. I didn't fully understand until I met my spiritual father, Apostle Marlon D. Hester, in 2009 when I was nineteen. By then, I was already tied up in a soul tie and deep in denial. Honestly, I didn't want to hear about it because, in my mind, "This is my man. My man, my man!" Whew, I was so wrong.

Nobody tells you that when you become intimate with someone, it can cost you a lot—especially your peace. And let's not talk about time. Time is valuable, and once it's gone, you can't get it back. In the moment, we don't think about that. We want what we want. But what I've learned is that if you don't pray about everything and seek God first, things probably won't go how you expected. God is a jealous God, and if anything pulls you away from Him, He'll allow things to happen just to get your attention.

When I operate outside of God's will, my life gets chaotic. I don't care how much I pray or fast—if it's not God's will, it's not going to work. Once I learned about soul ties, I recognized that I was in one. And when you're locked in with someone mentally, emotionally, and physically, it's hard to break free.

So how did I break free after years in a relationship that wasn't right for me? I had to take accountability. I sat with myself, apologized to God for giving my heart to someone else instead of Him, and made the choice to do better. I realized I was investing in something God never ordained. Enough was enough.

I made a confession. I forgave. I apologized to God and to myself. And I remembered that my story needed to happen. I couldn't go back to something unfruitful. I had already wasted enough time.

I truly believe God allows pain on purpose—because there is purpose in pain. God is a gentleman. He gives us free will. But our choices either align with His plan or our own. That's why you can't plan your life by yourself—what you want may not be what God wants for you.

Once God starts healing your heart, you must be careful. You can't go back to the things He delivered you from. Healing is a process. It doesn't happen overnight. You have to surrender and let God lead completely.

In my healing journey, I was still vulnerable. That's why I had to seek God daily—even if it meant waking up earlier, praying, worshipping, and reading His Word. But I also had to be careful not to let work, mentoring, working out, and other passions get in the way of my time with God. Anything you put before Him, He'll interrupt.

I'm on this journey for a better life—spiritually, mentally, emotionally. I thought about my niece, cousins, students, and mentees. It's pressure being a role model, but it also inspired me to keep going.

I always understood the importance of purity, even though I broke that commitment. But I also knew I wasn't going to give my body to just anyone. I'd already been through too much. During my healing, I didn't want to let any man in—unless he was sent by God.

Still, I wouldn't be real if I didn't talk about my son—birthed in the middle of my healing. Energy is real. And I'm big on who I allow in my space. When I met my son's father, we were both healing. We clicked and connected instantly, but I lost sight of God again. I let a good thing become a distraction from the best thing: my time with God.

And that's where I went wrong—again. You have to pray about everything and everyone you allow in your life. The timing was off. And when you move ahead of God, things get chaotic. I don't regret my son—he's a blessing—but I do regret moving ahead of God.

Even in our mess, God can produce a blessing. Do I wish some things were different? Sure. But I can't change the past. I can only grow from it. Nobody is perfect. What matters most is growth. If you're not learning from your experiences, that's the real problem.

Yes, life is hard—especially when you live for God. You're judged more. There was a time I cared about what people thought. Not anymore. I embrace all of me—my highs, lows, wins, and failures. What I care about now is fulfilling my purpose, leading people to God, being a great mother, daughter, mentor, and woman of God.

I'm not ashamed of my mistakes. If I didn't go through what I did, how could I help others? I'm not perfect and never will be. But every day I ask God for more of Him and less of me.

Now I speak up. I share my story because someone needs to hear it. Life isn't easy. But with God, you can stand.

I don't sugarcoat anything. When you're real, people feel safe. They see your humanity and open up. Your honesty can help someone else heal. That's what authenticity does—it builds real connections.

So if you're turning your pain into purpose, do this:

Acknowledge what you've been through.

Let yourself feel it.

Process it.

Reflect on what you've learned.

Find your strength.

Use your story to help others.

 And most importantly—let God lead your life.

You might fall, but get back up and go even harder. God's got you. He will never leave you or forsake you.

Build your relationship with Him. Seek Him daily—even if it's just 30 minutes. Stay consistent. Pray about everything—even the little things like which grocery store to go to. Yes, it's that serious.

Never put anyone or anything before God. He should always be first.

I'll leave you with one of my favorite scriptures:

Proverbs 3:5 — "Trust in the Lord with all your heart, and lean not to your own understanding; in all your ways acknowledge Him, and He will direct your path."

Chapter 6

YOU ARE WORTHY A HOLISTIC JOURNEY TO HEALTH AND HEALING

Jacquia Paul, a medicine woman rooted in the vibrant pulse or Brooklyn, NY where she lives with her husband and two sons. Brooklyn has been her sanctuary, the crucible of her transformation since the 90's. A biologist by training, she perceives life's intricate dance as a sacred text, deciphering its wisdom through the lens of holistic healing and self-development. Her practice is a profound alchemy, where scientific rigor converges with the timeless cadence of ancient wisdom.

As a certified life coach, yoga instructor, and-wellness teacher, she dedicates herself to serving her community, crafting immersive wellness experiences-meditation and sound baths-that illuminate pathways to inner harmony.

Jacquia Paul

REBORN FROM THE WRECKAGE: A HOLISTIC JOURNEY TO WHOLENESS

The Beginning of Becoming

There are moments in life when the mirror no longer reflects who you are. Instead, it reveals the woman you've survived being. And when I say survived, I mean the version of me that learned to stay quiet when she wanted to scream. The one who smiled on cue, performed strength like it was second nature, and carried pain in her body like it was part of her DNA. I've had to unlearn all of that. I was a child born into chaos; into a world that didn't feel safe, where love was inconsistent and stability was a fantasy. I learned to read the energy in the room before I even knew how to read words. Survival became second nature. I learned how to disappear in plain sight. And while on the outside I seemed like the "good girl," the "strong one," the one who had it all together, inside I was holding my breath every day. I was a girl with big dreams; creative, curious, and spiritually sensitive but that version of me got buried under the noise, the trauma, the generational curses that nobody around me had the tools to break. My body carried the residue of every unspoken hurt, every time I was dismissed, overlooked, touched without permission, or asked to be someone I wasn't. And yet, somehow, I still held on to a tiny flicker of light inside.

When I became a woman, that same little girl was still inside me, screaming to be heard. I became a mother and a wife, carrying everyone's needs while mine stayed buried. I went years without tending to my soul. I was holding it together, yes but at what cost?

I wasn't living. I was performing. And I was in pain—not just emotionally, but physically. My body became a messenger for all the things I was too afraid to say out loud.

I didn't just wake up one day healed. No. I woke up fighting. Fighting for air. For clarity. For me. Healing wasn't cute. It wasn't linear. It was raw, spiritual, physical, and deeply emotional. I had to confront everything I once suppressed. I had to grieve the versions of myself I performed just to make other people comfortable. I had to stop shrinking, even when that made others uncomfortable. Especially then. My healing didn't happen in isolation. It happened in the mess. In the middle of motherhood. In my marriage. In the ache of chronic pain. It happened when I stopped waiting for permission to reclaim my body, my truth, my joy. It happened when I stopped trying to be the version of myself that made other people feel safe and started becoming the version that made me feel free.

This is not a story about tragedy. It's a story about triumph. It's about the woman I'm becoming not whole, holy, and no longer afraid to take up space. It's about trusting my voice, even when it shakes. It's about alchemizing pain into power. It's about knowing that I don't owe anyone a watered-down version of myself. I am not just healing—I'm becoming. And in that becoming, I've found peace. Not the kind that comes from outside validation, but the kind that comes when you finally return home to yourself.

A BRAIN CONDITION AND A HEAVY HEART

I was born with Chiari malformation—a rare neurological condition where part of the brain pushes into the spinal canal. The diagnosis itself sounded like something out of a textbook, but for me, it's always been deeply personal. From the beginning, the odds were stacked against me. The doctors told my mother I might never walk, never function, never live what they called a "normal" life. But even then, before I had language or memory, I defied the narrative. Because I was never meant to be normal. I was born to be extraordinary.

Still, let's be real—living with Chiari hasn't been easy. It's been painful. It's been exhausting. The headaches weren't just headaches—they were migraines that took me out of my body. My neck would stiffen so badly I'd feel paralyzed. My balance was unreliable. My nervous system constantly on edge. My body, from a young age, carried a weight it never asked for. While other kids were playing and running free, I was managing symptoms I didn't even have words for yet.

But that physical pain wasn't the only thing I carried.

I was also born into a lineage of unspoken grief. A family stitched together with secrets, survival mechanisms, and wounds that were passed down like heirlooms. In my house, love was often conditional, and silence was the language we spoke fluently. I learned very quickly that to be accepted, I had to stay quiet. Smile. Be good. Don't ask too many questions. Don't take up too much space. I watched women in my family—especially my mother—carry the weight of everything without ever putting it down. And I followed suit.

My mother was a fighter, no doubt. She did the best she could with what she had. But she was also deeply wounded. And so much of my childhood was spent reading her emotions, trying to stabilize her when I barely knew how to steady myself. I often felt like I was mothering my mother—taking care of her emotionally, managing her stress, learning how to make myself invisible when needed. That kind of emotional labor ages you fast.

I thought strength meant pushing through. I thought it meant pretending I was okay when I wasn't. I thought it meant never breaking down, never crying, never needing too much from anyone. But all that pretending started to rot me from the inside out. My body was screaming, and no one could hear it because I was so good at hiding it. I was so good at performing strength, I forgot what softness felt like.

But the truth is, healing doesn't happen through silence or perfection. Healing happens when you fall apart. When you stop holding your breath and let yourself breathe, even if it's through the tears. I had to give myself permission to unravel—to stop being "strong" long enough to actually feel, grieve, and let go. And that's where I began to rebuild. Piece by sacred piece.

I began to understand that strength isn't in how much pain you can hold—it's in your willingness to release it. It's in your ability to forgive yourself for the times you didn't know better, but still hoped for better. So yes, I was born with a brain condition. But I was also born with a brave heart. A sensitive soul. And a purpose bigger than my pain. I don't exist to survive. I'm here to transform.

SILENT SCARS AND SURVIVAL

Abuse doesn't just break you—it reshapes you. It gets under your skin and burrows into your nervous system. It teaches you to read people's moods before they speak, to anticipate danger even when none is present. It trains you to ignore your own needs, your own voice, your own truth—just to keep the peace. Just to be safe.

I grew up walking on eggshells, always adjusting, always calculating how to take up less space. I became a master at self-abandonment. Hiding my feelings wasn't a choice—it was survival. I didn't want to upset anyone. I didn't want to be "too sensitive." I didn't want to be the reason someone else exploded. So I shrunk. I made myself easy to ignore. My presence quieted. My voice became a whisper. And the thing is, once you learn how to disappear emotionally, it's hard to come back to yourself. At 15, I met my father for the first time. For years, I had built him up in my head. He was this mystery, this missing piece I thought might make me feel whole. I thought maybe, just maybe, he'd show up and love me in a way that would undo all the hurt. But when he came, he was emotionally unavailable—present in body but distant in every other way. The fantasy I had created unraveled, and I was left holding more questions than comfort. His presence didn't fill the holes—it echoed them.

I realized then that even the things we long for can still leave us empty. That blood doesn't always equal bond. That sometimes, the deepest ache comes from someone who was never truly there to begin with. Family gatherings didn't bring relief—they reminded me of the ways I didn't belong. I often felt like a guest in my own bloodline, an outsider trying to be "enough" to be included. I laughed at jokes that didn't land. I

showed up when I didn't want to. I gave more than I received. All in the hope that maybe, this time, I'd feel chosen.

That longing for acceptance followed me into adulthood like a shadow. It showed up in my friendships, in my mothering, and especially in my marriage. I carried an invisible checklist of how to keep people from leaving. Be quiet. Be helpful. Be everything they need. Don't be too emotional. Don't be too demanding. Stay small. Stay sweet.

But I was never meant to stay small. I was never meant to carry the weight of everyone else's comfort at the expense of my own.

Looking back, I can see how much of my life was shaped by that desperate search for worthiness. Not because I didn't have worth—but because I was conditioned to believe I had to earn it. Through silence. Through service. Through suffering.

But that story? I'm rewriting it.

I'm learning that my worth doesn't come from how well I endure pain or perform perfection. It comes from the simple, undeniable fact that I exist. That I breathe. That I'm here.

Survival shaped me—but it no longer defines me. It molded me to be the thriver that I am today!

Let me know if you'd like to connect this into Page 4, or if you want to include a transitional paragraph about how motherhood or your spiritual awakening began shifting this mindset. You're writing a whole truth, and it's powerful.

MARRIAGE, MOTHERHOOD, AND THE MIRROR

I married young, holding tightly to the idea that love would finally save me. I thought if I could just build something stable, something solid, something different from what I came from, it would quiet all the ache inside me. I was chasing safety. Chasing home. Chasing the version of love I had always longed for but never fully received.

We built a life. Had children. Bought furniture, celebrated birthdays, took photos that looked like joy. And from the outside, it all appeared to be in place. A picture-perfect family. A woman with a husband, kids, and responsibilities. A life most people would envy.

But inside? I was disappearing.

Slowly, silently, I started to lose myself. I couldn't see it at first—it crept in quietly. At first, it was the small things. My voice getting softer. My needs taking a backseat. The hobbies I once loved slipping away. The dreams I used to talk about getting filed under "maybe one day." I didn't even notice how much I was shrinking because I was too busy trying to hold it all together.

Marriage became a mirror. One I couldn't look away from. It reflected all the ways I had abandoned myself. All the wounds I hadn't healed. All the little girl parts of me that were still hoping to be rescued. I kept waiting for love to feel like freedom, but more often than not, it felt like suffocation. I was walking on eggshells again—this time in my own home.

Motherhood was another mirror. It cracked me open in ways I wasn't prepared for. Loving my children so deeply made me realize just how little of that love I had ever given to myself. I poured into them endlessly, all while running on empty. I wanted to be the mother I never had. To give them a version of childhood I was denied. And in doing so, I forgot that I was still someone's child too—still deserving of care, of rest, of gentleness.

There were days I would stand in the mirror and not recognize the woman looking back at me. She was tired. Tense. Holding back tears. Stretching herself thin to keep the peace. She had learned to put everyone else first, and somewhere along the way, she forgot she mattered too.

I stayed longer than I should have. I silenced my truth for the sake of stability. I convinced myself that things would get better, that if I just loved harder, tried harder, prayed harder—it would all fall into place. But love shouldn't feel like a battlefield. And peace shouldn't come at the cost of your soul. Eventually, the pain became too loud to ignore. The ache in my body. The weight in my chest. The tension in my spirit. My body was telling the truth I was too afraid to speak. That I was unfulfilled. That I was unseen. That I had outgrown the space I had once begged to fit into.

Marriage didn't save me. Motherhood didn't complete me. What did? Facing myself. Telling the truth. Peeling back the layers and choosing, finally, to stop abandoning me.

The mirror no longer shows me a woman who's lost. It shows me a woman who left nothing of herself behind. A woman who's rising—not perfect, but present. Not silent, but sovereign. This is what reclamation looks like.

HEALING IN PIECES

Healing didn't come in some perfect package, tied with a bow and delivered to my doorstep. It came in pieces—scattered across years of my life. Some pieces I had to dig deep for. Other times , I found myself on the floor, breathless, barely holding on. It didn't look pretty. It looked like therapy sessions where I sat in silence because I didn't know where to begin. It looked like crying during yoga because my body remembered things my mouth still couldn't say. It looked like writing in my journal at 3am, trying to make sense of the weight I carried.

It came through the moments I started choosing me. Like taking long walks with tears rolling down my cheeks, not wiping them away for once. Saying no when I wanted to, even if my voice shook. Turning off my phone and giving myself permission to rest—not because I earned it, but because I needed it. Because I deserved it.

The more I began honoring myself, the more healing found its way in. Slowly, I started to trust my own voice again. To believe that maybe I didn't have to keep carrying everything. Maybe I didn't have to prove my worth through pain. Maybe I could put some things down.

Setting boundaries? That changed everything. I had to learn that protecting my peace wasn't selfish—it was sacred. It was medicine. I let go of people who only loved the version of me that stayed small. I stopped explaining my choices to people committed to misunderstanding me. That part was hard. But necessary. Because the truth is, I couldn't fully step into my healing while still clinging to the things that broke me.

I found my way back to myself through holistic healing. Through reiki sessions where I finally felt seen without having to say a word. Through sound baths that calmed my nervous system and reminded me that peace wasn't a myth—it was my birthright. Through the quiet magic of herbalism, where the plants taught me to trust in divine timing, in cycles, in rest. Through meditation, where I sat with my breath and listened—to my body, to my spirit, to the parts of me that had been waiting for years to be acknowledged. And then there was science. Studying biology and the brain gave me the language for what my soul already knew. I finally understood why I always felt so tense, so tired, so "on." Trauma lives in the body. It wires the nervous system to survive, not to thrive. And I had been surviving for so long, I didn't even know what thriving looked like.

But the moment everything shifted was when I met her. My inner child who had experienced childhood sexual molestation. That little girl with the big eyes and even bigger dreams. The one who tried so hard to be perfect. To be good. To be enough. She didn't need fixing. She needed love. So I held her. I rocked her. I let her be messy. I let her cry for everything she never got to grieve. I told her, "You didn't imagine it. It happened. But you're safe now. I've got us."

And in that moment, I didn't just heal—I came home to myself.

That's what healing has been for me. Not one big breakthrough, but a thousand quiet moments of choosing myself again and again. One piece at a time. And now, when I look at the woman I'm becoming, I see her wholeness. Not because nothing ever broke her—but because she picked up every single piece and loved herself through the process.

RECLAIMING ME, WITHOUT LETTING GO OF EVERYTHING

There's a quiet kind of revolution that happens when a woman decides to remember herself. Not out of rage. Not out of rebellion. But through reflection. Through those still, sacred moments where she finally stops silencing the whispers in her spirit. That's where I found myself—standing in the middle of motherhood, marriage, and memory, holding the forgotten pieces of me I had long tucked away to keep the peace.

I was never trying to be difficult. I just wanted to be whole. But I kept shrinking, folding, adjusting—until I barely recognized the woman I had become.

Being married as an American woman to a St. Lucian man brought a blend of beauty and friction. His culture was rich in family, pride, and tradition. His roots ran deep—anchored in an island life where women

were often expected to be soft-spoken, sacrificial, always standing beside their men, never in front. Meanwhile, I was raised in a country that told me the opposite: Be bold. Be independent. Make your own way. Speak up. Don't shrink for anyone. I believed in that. At least, I used to.

Somewhere along the way, that fire dimmed. Not because I stopped believing, but because I got tired. Tired of trying to live in two worlds at once. Tired of translating my needs into a language that felt foreign in my own home. I became the peacekeeper, the planner, the provider of emotional safety. I played the role. The good wife. The strong mom. The glue. The healer. The everything.

And still, I felt invisible.

Our home wasn't loud with arguments all the time—it was heavy with what went unsaid. Heavy with expectations I never agreed to, but still carried. He loved me in the way he knew how. He showed up. He worked hard. He provided. But I needed more than provision. I needed presence. I needed depth. I needed a partner who didn't just love what I did, but loved who I was—even when I wasn't doing anything. So, I began to choose me. Not all at once. Not with ultimatums or dramatic exits. But slowly. Quietly. And unapologetically. I started going where I felt light, doing things I forget was enjoyable like hanging out with friends. Where I felt seen. I stopped asking for permission to exist in my fullness. I let myself soften again; not to please, but to feel. I stopped explaining my dreams, defending my boundaries, or justifying my decisions. I stopped abandoning myself in the name of love.

This wasn't about leaving. It was about leading—my life, my healing, my joy.

I wanted my sons to see it. To see a woman choose herself without bitterness. To see that wholeness doesn't require anyone else to break. I wanted to teach them that love can exist even when it's imperfect. Even when it's being reimagined. Even when it's being redefined in real time.

And the truth is, I don't know where this road is leading. I recognize that sometimes marriages outgrow their original form. That what once fit no longer aligns. We're at a crossroads. And while I still love him, I love me more now. Enough to pause. Enough to pray. Enough to trust that God will lead me in the most purposeful direction—one that honors both my healing and my peace.

Because choosing yourself doesn't always mean walking away. Sometimes, it just means coming home to who you were before the world told you to be someone else.

RISING IN PURPOSE

At some point in my journey, I realized—I wasn't just healing for me anymore. I was healing for my lineage. For my children. For every woman who had ever been told she was too much, too broken, too

loud, too soft, too complicated to rise. And once I tapped into that, something inside me shifted. I began to create again—not out of desperation, but from divine inspiration.

I opened my heart and my hands to wellness entrepreneurship. Not just to make money, but to make meaning. I knew I had something to give. Something sacred. I started small— making herbal supplements, bottling herbal teas in my kitchen, mixing remedies from ancestral wisdom, sharing little healing moments on Instagram. What started as a whisper turned into a wave. I hosted sound baths and yoga sessions, ran community wellness workshops, and poured my soul into every offering.

My business became an extension of my heart. A living, breathing altar to everything I had survived and everything I now stood for. Every product I made, every session I led, every post I wrote—it all came from the most honest, grounded place within me. I wasn't trying to be perfect. I was trying to be real. And that realness? That's what people connected to.

Even on days when my Chiari flared up—when my neck stiffened, when the migraines came rushing in—I kept showing up. Sometimes that looked like a full class of students breathing with me. Other times, it looked like resting in my healing room with my eyes closed and a heating pad on my back. But I didn't quit. I just adjusted. I gave myself grace.

I stopped waiting for the "right time" or the perfect version of me to arrive. I started showing up as I was. And in doing that, I gave other women permission to do the same. To start where they were. To heal while still hurting. To build while still grieving. To rise while still remembering.

I used my voice—online, in sessions, and now, here in this book. And every time I shared a piece of my story, I felt something sacred crack open. My vulnerability became someone else's lifeline. My truth became someone else's permission slip. Every post, every story, every product I created became a seed planted in someone else's garden of hope. And the beauty of it all? Those seeds grew. I began hearing from women who said, "I feel seen because of you." "You reminded me that healing is possible." "Your story helped me believe in my own again." That's when I knew—I was walking in purpose. Not because everything was easy or perfectly aligned, but because I was finally in alignment with myself. Rising in purpose hasn't meant that all the pain disappeared. It's meant I learned how to alchemize it. To turn the grief into guidance, the breakdowns into breakthroughs, the trauma into truth. This is the work I was born to do. This is the season of becoming the woman my younger self needed—and my future self is proud of.

I'm not just building a business. I'm building a legacy. I'm building community. I'm building wholeness.

PAGE 8: BOUNDARIES AND BECOMING

As I healed, I became more sensitive—to energy, to alignment, to the whispers of my body and the vibrations in every room I entered. My spirit could no longer tolerate what it once accepted out of survival. What used to feel familiar started to feel heavy. Conversations, connections, environments—if they weren't in alignment with my healing, they started to drain me. I had to protect my peace like it was my only possession. Sometimes, it was.

That's when boundaries became my new language. At first, they felt foreign—like fences I wasn't sure I had the right to build. But I kept at it. I stopped

over-explaining my "no." I stopped apologizing for needing space, for outgrowing roles that once defined me, for walking away from people who made me feel like I was both too much and not enough at the same time.

I stopped chasing closure. I stopped chasing people, period.

I started listening to my body instead. To the tension in my shoulders that showed up every time I ignored a red flag. To the headaches that followed conversations where I betrayed my truth. To the calm that came when I finally said no without guilt. My body had always been trying to speak to me—I just hadn't known how to listen. Now, I lead with that intuition. I honor it.

I began to sit in solitude without shame. What used to feel like loneliness became sacred space. Silence became my sanctuary. I no longer feared being alone, because I had finally come home to myself. I realized that solitude isn't punishment—it's preparation. It's where I recharge, where I reconnect with God, where I remember who I am beneath all the noise.

I forgave myself for staying too long in places that bruised me. I stopped judging the version of me who didn't know better. She wanted better. She was doing the best she could with the tools she had. And now? I honor her by continuing to grow. By making the hard choices she was too afraid to make. By living in the freedom she only dreamed of.

I'm still learning. Still softening. Still shedding layers of who I had to be just to survive. But now, I do it rooted in self-love, not shame. I don't hustle for healing anymore—I let it unfold, I let it rise. I let it teach me.

I move from a place of knowing—knowing that my story matters. My truth matters. My body, my voice, my presence—they all matter. And this healing? This becoming? It's holy.

Because I'm not just becoming a new version of myself. I'm remembering who I've been all along. I'm not broken—I'm blooming. I'm not lost—I'm becoming.

And that becoming? It's the most sacred thing I've ever done.

THE LEGACY I'M LIVING

Today, I show up for my sons not just as their mother—but as a whole woman. That right there is the legacy I'm building. They don't just see me making dinner or doing drop-offs or helping with homework. They see me in my becoming. They see a woman who refuses to settle. A woman who is still dreaming, still growing, still standing even after being knocked down more times than she can count. They've watched me struggle, but more importantly, they've watched me rise. They've seen me cry in one breath and speak affirmations in the next. They've seen me lay down because of the pain—and then get back up because of the purpose and dedication as a mother. They've seen me create, rest, release, and reimagine my life in real time.

I don't want them to grow up thinking love means sacrifice without limits. I want them to know that love is rooted in truth. That a woman who loves herself is not a threat—she's a blessing. I want them to understand that strength is not silence, and softness is not weakness.

They are learning what love really looks like—not the performative kind that shows up in public but withholds in private. Not perfection that crumbles under pressure. But presence. Patience. Power. They're learning that it's okay to change. That healing is ongoing. That joy is a practice. That boundaries are love in action.

When they look at me, they don't just see "mom." They see a woman rebuilding her life from the inside out. A woman who took her pain and turned it into purpose. A woman who was born into trauma but chose transformation instead. The legacy I'm living doesn't begin with what broke me. It begins with what I decided to become in spite of it.

They won't inherit silence or shame from me. They'll inherit the truth. They'll inherit emotional literacy. They'll inherit a mother who wasn't perfect, but who was present. A mother who modeled what it means to keep going. To keep growing.

My past no longer defines me. My purpose does. And through that purpose, I'm planting seeds in my sons that will grow long after I'm gone. Seeds of self-love, respect, empathy, and vision. Because the real legacy? It's not what we leave behind—it's how we show up now.

And I choose to show up fully. Authentically. Unapologetically. For them. For me. For all the women in my bloodline who never got the chance.

THRIVING, NOT JUST SURVIVING

This isn't a fairytale. There was no magic wand. No perfect savior. No clean ending tied with a bow. Healing is messy. It's layered. Some days still hurt. Some triggers still sting. And the pain didn't vanish just because I chose growth. But every single day, I make the choice to thrive. Not just exist. Not just get by. Not just check boxes. I choose to live—on purpose, with purpose.

I am not the girl who stayed silent to keep the peace. I am not the woman who stayed small to be accepted. I am not the version of myself that broke just to make others whole. I am the warrior who rose. I am the woman who walked through fire and came out wrapped in light.

I found my voice—and it's louder than fear. I found my worth—and it's no longer up for debate. I found the divine not in some distant place or someone else's validation—but right here, in my own reflection. I found God in the mirror, in the stillness, in the softness I once called weakness.

To every woman who's still in the fire: I see you. I know the weight you're carrying. I know the war between staying and saving yourself. I know the ache of feeling invisible in spaces you've poured yourself into. But hear me clearly—you are not alone. You are not broken. You are becoming.

Keep going. Keep walking through the discomfort. Keep choosing yourself, even when it costs you things you thought you couldn't live without. Keep crying if you need to, but never stop rising. Because every step you take toward healing creates a path for another woman to follow. Your freedom is not just for you—it's a blueprint. A light in the dark for someone else still searching for their way home.

And to myself—to the woman who kept showing up even when it felt like no one saw her... I am proud of you. You did it. You made it. Not because the road was easy—but because you never gave up. You turned your pain into power. You stopped running from yourself and finally turned inward. You chose you. You broke cycles. You reclaimed your name. You remembered your divinity.

This is not the end. This is just the beginning.

You are not just surviving anymore.

You are thriving.

MINI HOLISTIC GUIDE: FROM SURVIVAL TO SOVEREIGNTY

This mini guide is for the woman who has carried it all—pain, silence, responsibility, shame—and is finally ready to carry herself with love and freedom. My healing didn't happen overnight. It wasn't a single ritual, conversation, or yoga pose. It was a commitment to coming back home to myself, again and again, even when I was exhausted, scared, or unsure.

Here are the holistic tools, rituals, and truths that supported my healing—and can support yours too.

1. Mind-Body-Spirit Practices: Yoga & Breathwork, Restorative yoga to release trauma stored in the body, Deep belly breathing and alternate nostril breathing to calm my nervous system

   - Gentle morning stretches when I couldn't move much from pain

   - Sound Healing(crystal bowls): Sound baths helped me reset emotionally and vibrationally

   - Reiki(energy healing): Reiki gave me peace when nothing else worked, I then became a Reiki practitioner. Energy healing cleared blocks I couldn't see but could always feel

   - Meditation & Visualization: Guided meditations to reconnect to my inner child

- Visualization techniques to see the version of me I was becoming Mantra: "I deserve to feel good in my body and safe in my truth."

2. Herbal & Natural Remedies

   - Homemade Herbal Products: Soaps, oils and butters with herbs like lavender, chamomile and peppermint

   - Herbal teas for womb healing, stress relief, and mental clarity like lemon balm and red raspberry

   - Natural remedies for my kids and myself instead of always turning to pharmaceuticals

   - Nutrition as Medicine: your kitchen is the farmacy

   - Anti-inflammatory foods to reduce pain (turmeric, ginger, greens)

   - Hydration with lemon water and herbal infusions

   - Listening to my body's needs instead of following diet trends

3. Emotional & Ancestral Healing

   - Journaling & Voice Notes

   - I started documenting my feelings out loud or in writing, especially when I felt misunderstood

   - I rewrote the narratives that were handed down to me from family, culture, or religion

   - Inner Child Work

- Connecting with the little girl inside me who just wanted to feel safe, heard, and protected

- Creating rituals of softness—bubble baths, dancing, crying without shame

- Letting myself be held, not just be the one who holds

- Therapy & Coaching

- Talking to someone who didn't try to fix me, just held space

- Life coaching helped me move from victim to visionary

4. Spiritual Awakening & Faith

- God & Intuition: Discovery new hopeful beliefs about life and metaphysics

- I stopped asking others for permission to live my truth

- I began praying in my own way—sometimes in silence, sometimes with tears, sometimes through movement

- I honored the divine within me, not just the God outside of me

- I gave myself permission to define love, motherhood, and marriage on my own terms.

- I learned: tradition is not always truth

- Culture should never come before my soul's peace

5. Reclaiming My Identity

- Beauty & Body Sovereignty

- I cut my hair and crowned myself in confidence

- I dressed for me—not for approval

- I gave myself permission to feel beautiful even when in pain

6. Boundaries & Boldness

- I stopped over-explaining, over-apologizing, and over-functioning

- I said "no" without guilt and "yes" to my joy

- I protected my peace like my life depended on it—because it did

Last words,

For the Woman Reading This:

- You don't have to be fully healed to start helping yourself.

- You don't need permission to reclaim your power.

- You are not broken—you are breaking through.

Start small today: light a candle. Take a deep breath. Speak your truth aloud. Touch your heart and say, I am worth the effort it takes to heal. And keep going.

Much love,
Coach Jay

Chapter 7

YOU'RE NOT CRAZY. YOU'RE CALLED

Tonekia Williams is a visionary, educator, author, entrepreneur, and philanthropist from Brooklyn, NY. With a BS in Psychology from Touro University, she leads with faith, authenticity, and transparency.

She's the author of Gratefully Broken and 14 Days of Prayer & Intimacy. Tonekia has co-authored 3 inner healing journey books; Unmute Yourself, From Hurt to Healing, and Tuesdays at 7. Lastly, her children's book, Hugg'n Bear Cares: Actions and Reactions, reflects her passion for social-emotional learning.

Tonekia Williams

As a special education teacher, Tonekia empowers her "little superheroes" with patience and purpose. She also founded Worldwide Hugs, a nonprofit that supports communities with meals, resources, and hope. Tonekia's mission is to help others heal and boldly embrace their purpose-one hug, one prayer, and one life at a time.

YOU'RE NOT CRAZY,
YOU'RE CALLED. HIS PLAN.

Laying It All Down

I laid on my prayer mat, desperately pleading with God to make me feel normal again. My mind was racing, and thoughts were physically bouncing around in my head. It always seemed like I was being attacked during transitional inclines. The closer I got to reaching my goals, the more I felt my mental health slipping.

There were so many days and nights I found myself internally battling. Was I really dealing with mental challenges, or was the enemy attacking my mind?

Please don't let that go over your head. I truly believe the power of life and death is in our words. You have to speak life over yourself constantly. What you speak into the atmosphere is what you'll eventually see.

Family, please stick with me. By the end of this chapter, we'll be releasing some issues that we have clung to. Shall we prepare to feel a little lighter after this experience?

Get your paper, pens, and boxes of tissues. We've got work to do.

What Are You Holding On To?

Before we proceed, let me ask you: have you been carrying or harboring anything that has been weighing you down? (Pause)

I'll go first. For the majority of my life, I've walked around with trauma, excuses, self-pity, and doubtful voices that became mental burdens. These mental burden's attempted to become part of my identity. So, I'll ask again—have you been walking around with anything that has become a false part of your identity? (I'll wait...)

Heyyyy Gurl, XoXo

Okay, okay, I know I've been a bit rude. I'm somewhat late, but everyone reading this chapter—we are now Sisters! I'm usually the family member who shows up late to the family gatherings and slips out early. I'll make it up to you by feeding you good food and listening to most of your problems. I'll also play the good tunes off my music playlist. (Yes, that includes all the 90s and early 2000 R&B. I'll even slip in the gospel, and Afrobeats).

Now that we're officially introduced, let's get into the good stuff.

BREAKING THE SILENCE

My journey might seem strange to some, but God molded us all differently for his purpose and glory. We are all created in his image to BREAK barriers and push past conventional thinking. Some folks are afraid to admit what they're struggling with. Others are ashamed to speak on what God has delivered them from.

But I refuse to let the enemy punk me. **My mama birthed a fighter.**

Spiritual warfare is real, and so are the feelings of doubt and confusion that come with it. My problem was bigger than me, I was fighting the stability of my mind. **This meant war.**

What Is Spiritual Warfare?

Spiritual warfare, according to the Bible, is the ongoing battle between good (God and His angels) and evil (Satan and his demons). **It's not a physical fight—it's spiritual**. It's the struggle to maintain faith, resist temptation, and stand firm against evil influences that try to distract, deceive, or destroy our relationship with God.

One of my favorite verses, John 10:10, says it best: *"The thief comes only to steal, kill, and destroy. I came that they may have life and have it abundantly."*

The plan is clear. It's up to us to recognize the enemy's schemes and dismantle them.

EQUIPPED THROUGH EXPERIENCE

When God gives me a topic to write or speak on, He also equips me through experience—sometimes painful ones. My wisdom from this area came with sleepless nights and asking God, *"Why me?"*

Only now do I understand the root and the solution. **After Praying and fasting**, I asked God. What should my topic in the HER'D anthology be? He answered by allowing me to focus on what I was battling with at the moment. I was lost for words. Honestly, I was being a bit bratty. I remember asking the father, you want me to put all my business out there huh? (LBS)

Matthew 11:28 says:

"Come to me, all you who are weary and burdened, and I will give you rest."

Then there's my favorite verse, Matthew 7:7:

"Ask and it will be given to you; seek and you will find; knock and the door will be opened to you."

Y'all, after reading these scriptures about 40 times, something clicked. A light bulb popped on and it had a whole voice. I thought to myself, *"I've been walking around with these silent conditions for too long. Why haven't I asked my Father for guidance?"*

That's when the game changed.

Detective Williams on the scene

I was on a mission, I started to investigate the strange patterns and outlandish behaviors in my family. Because obviously, these conditions didn't drop from the sky. So where did they come from? Many of us didn't have our priorities together and seemed to struggle with confusion or mental instability. **Once I started digging, I discovered cycles—abnormal ones.**

Call me Detective Williams—I was about to crack the case!

In my memoir *Gratefully Broken*, I spoke candidly about my relationship with my mom. Her life was full of trauma—exposure to drugs, physical, sexual, and emotional abuse. Before her, my grandmother had also endured pain as well—abuse, and the loss of three sons before the age of 30. Not to mention, a complicated marriage that left her running out of state, fleeing with her young children.

On my grandfather's side, there were whispers of mental complications. His family was stable citizens who possessed great careers and owned homes. Still, there were elephants in the room. In many urban communities, we sweep those conversations under the rug.

Let's normalize talking about the uncomfortable stuff. My personal challenge was mental health. Maybe yours is adultery, sexual molestation, witchcraft, daddy issues, struggles with sexuality, or abnormal disorders. However, What we don't acknowledge will eventually haunt us. SPEAK UP!

I use to joke and say, *"If my family is crazy, what do you think I am?"* Little did I know, I was partnering with the enemy. **My words had power, and I was using them to curse myself.**

THE DAY EVERYTHING CHANGED

In 2009, my world shifted. My grandmother—the woman who raised me—was found unconscious in her home. She was a praying woman, full of love. That day, I had a strange feeling after work and skipped happy hour to go home and check on Granny. That evening, I found her cold and lifeless on our bathroom floor. To this day, it still feels surreal. After that, my attitude towards life was tainted. **I inherited the weight she carried**—the dysfunction, the trauma, the chaos. Fast forward to 2012. I call that chapter of my life "Best Dressed Yet, Broken." On the outside, I was polished—thanks to Granny and Mom, their styles were impeccable—but inside, I was a complete mess. As I grew up, I self-reflected. I noticed that my perception of myself was hideous. Often, I masked how I felt by striving to be the best dressed in the room. I didn't think I was smart, pretty or socially appealing. However, the outfit and shoes would come through for me every time. My way of thinking was negative and affected my wellbeing. In consequence, my decision making was poor. I forced myself on people due to the fact I did not feel adequate of maintaining genuine connections. **Even though I knew better, I kept choosing what hurt me.** I was simply existing, not living. **I wore my circumstances, tragedies and bloodline like a badge of honor.**

A NEW SEASON,

I didn't want to be a victim of my circumstances anymore. Still, healing didn't come overnight. **Even after my awakening, I stayed in turmoil for over a decade.** After grandma passed, I moved out on my own at 21. I stayed in that apartment for seven years. Biblically, the number seven represents completion. The soundtrack of my life was on repeat. **Grandma wasn't around to save me from all my alter-ego.** Sis, was in full effect. The daddy issues, the abandonment, and the insecurities had merged and were outside to play. Things had got a little deeper, these issues would negatively add to my self-esteem and value of myself, It all stemmed from what I thought was mental incapabilities. **While I was drowning and gasping for air, life didn't stop. I was officially the referee, public defender and counselor.** Unfortunately, my role was the glue holding all the madness together. Aiding with tantrums, spiraling addictions, mental hospital visits and fights were now on my skill list. But in 2019, something changed.

STILL BECOMING.

I met someone who helped me grow closer to God. She was an answered prayer. That relationship was only for a season, but the impact is going to last a lifetime. We shared a desire to strengthen our faith and understood the power of prayer.

John 15:7 says:

"If you abide in me, and my words abide in you, ask whatever you wish, and it will be done for you."

Mark 11:24 adds:

"Therefore I tell you, whatever you ask in prayer, believe that you have received it, and it will be yours."

Let me ask you—have you really been asking God for what you need? Or have you been carrying cycles like a new luxury purse. Are you holding onto things you were never meant to bear?

When I realized I was a child of the King, something broke. Once you accept Christ as your Lord and Savior you don't have to beg for freedom, it's your right. God doesn't want us in bondage so he sent his son to carry the cross. He wants us to come to Him like children and drop our burdens at His feet—like it's hot.

READY TO FIGHT.

I began taking mental inventory of my most challenging times. It always included intrusive, dark and fixated thoughts. I felt tired, grumpy, and antisocial 90% of the time. These were totally symptoms of depression and anxiety—**but I refused to diagnose**

myself. According to 2024 statistics, 57.8 million adults suffered from mental illness, with anxiety-related disorders being the most common. I'm not denying that many of us are fighting real mental health battles—but deep in my spirit. **I knew I wasn't just battling emotions. This was spiritual**.

I'm from New York, usually when we start a story we say Ok, so BOOM. Y'all ready for this?

Ok, so BOOM. After meeting my new friend she taught me more than expected. My life honestly took a spiritual incline and mental free-fall. I'm sure that doesn't make sense but I have something to tell you all. My grandmother raised me in church, when my mom was outside from Thursday to Monday, granny had me in God's house. I was on the usher board and choir. As I got older, like most I strayed away and did my own thing. **Eventually, I decided to get back in line and follow Christ, I visited many churches chasing his presence**. Little did I know the holy spirit was inside of me and wherever I went I wasn't alone. Feel-good churches started to become common. Truthfully, those churches keep you in sin and bondage. As believers, we need conviction. We can't go around living however we please. At some churches, I would listen to the pastor preach and sing hymns. **When I left and got home, I would continue to suffer with internal problems.** My remedy was silencing them momentarily with liquor, sex and binge eating. **Those churches never taught me how to fight spiritually.**

SQUARE UP, DON'T BLANK!

I had no idea what was in store. During the pandemic, life started to life! Just like millions, I was forced to deal with my problems, alone. While undergoing a global crisis. **All my shortcomings started to arise**. My new Sister in Christ, let's call her Monique, was an angel in human form. After many conversations and group chats. She was leading myself and other women to a brighter light with her ministry. We would have different conversations about topics we didn't feel comfortable telling others. **This was a safe space, a genuine sisterhood**. Monique had so much wisdom. Her friends were also fighters in the spirit and bomb boss babes. God had set me up for greatness and I was excited to explore this new role. **For 6 months I was isolated and alone during the pandemic.** It was literally me and God. The bible group chats and in person fellowships equipped me. **Most of our problems were the result of generational curses**, spiritual attacks, and stubborn demons that wanted our promises from God to fail. **To be brutally honest, I was dealing with ancestral curses**. I started to take more inventory. What was evident in my family, what cycles were clearly visible. Then, I aggressively started to pray against these issues. These demonic systems had been around longer than I could have ever imagined. **This battle wasn't solely mine**. Still, I had to knuckle up and prepare to fight. **How do you fight the unseen or unspoken?** In Mark 9, **Jesus told his disciples that certain demons would only come out through prayer and fasting**. These principles also inspired me to write my prayer journal; "14 days of prayer and intimacy". A women's devotional.

IDENTIFY & ATTACK THE SOURCE.

"Girl, you better pray and worship like you are crazy. Confuse the enemy". I'll never forget those words. At that time, I had exhausted all resources. Beyond the inner turmoil, solitude, and paranoia. I was depleted. **I would journal and meditate to identify issues. Then I would ask God for clarity on what I needed to pray against.** There were also times when I lacked faith and relied on the culture. For example, vividly I remember when demons started to fight against me. As long as you're oblivious, the kingdom of darkness will keep letting you think you are in control. When they are aware you know your authority, life changes. There was outward warfare. At this time, I would hear things in my home while I was alone and sometimes, I would see weird figures. My prayers seemed like that weren't enough. Do you believe I had the nerve to get sage and called myself getting rid of the spirits? As you can imagine, the spirits laughed at me and intensified. That's when I knew, I had to lock in with fasting and prayer. Shortly after, I did some research on YouTube university. **I wanted to know everything about fasting, the benefits of the sacrifice and prayers that coincided with the act.** Then, after all the information was gathered. During my alone time with the father, I prayed and asked to be led with the time frame and amount of days to fast. My results navigated me too fast for 10 days, from 12am to 6pm. I abstained from food and social media, praying every hour. Some of my prayers were conditioned around my mental health, my brain function, fixated thoughts, cleaning of my surroundings, breaking free from generational curses, being aligned with my purpose and being connected to more prayerful women. **In due time, I would receive vivid detailed dreams**

and clarity. This wasn't the ending of turmoil, however the beginning of a fasted intentional life of sacrifice to God. In return he started to heal me little by little.

Not so much of a fun fact; however, I'll share what God did for me through another fast. During the pandemic, Life had another unexpected turn. Which left me clinging to my only source, God. **I was in the midst of a horrible breakup that came with warning**. Every red flag that was ever created was visible, still. Sis wanted to test the water. In return, **I left that relationship wounded, confused, misled and a victim of black magic**. Let's take a moment and praise God for my sanity, cause I fought for my life. Honestly, I thought my life was over, this is how I know God is real. You probably wouldn't believe me. However, I fasted like my life depended on it. Maybe, because it did. **For 60 days, it was me, my bible, my prayer mat and GOD**. As you can see, **I was fighting a multitude of assignments from the enemy.** Inner indifferences, Generational curses, family trauma, mental imbalances, insecurities, abandonment issues and the list could go on. Let me proceed to share 1 last tangible jewel with you. **God was revealing his presence and the evidence of the demonic spirits connected to my mind.**

THE FINAL SAY;

When a person prays a great deal, they become sensitive to their environment. **The more you pray, your intimacy unlocks favor with God.** You also feel and see things others can't. This may sound out of the ordinary. However, being a kingdom kid has its benefits. In the Bible Jesus and his disciples healed the sick and casted out demons. In order to move forward they had to spend time in prayer with God. By his grace and mercy, Jesus did his will in human form on earth. **Moral of this passage: prayer, fasting and intimacy with God unlocks spiritual gifts**. Stay with me. I'm going somewhere special. We're about to land this plane.

Recalling back, I always thought I was what people called "physic." All along it was the Holy spirit leading me. I learned in order to have spiritual gifts you had to sacrifice. **We are sacrificing to the kingdom of God or the kingdom of darkness (choose wisely).** However, I've only sacrificed to God! I wanted to remain on the bright side of things. In all seriousness, the holy spirit always came right on time with warning. My body gave off signals when I was in danger. Have you ever been around people or in a specific setting and it felt unsafe? In your mind you say, let me get away from this person or out this area. Yup, that's the Holy Spirit and you better listen up!

THIS IS MAKING SENSE.

For the last six months of 2024, I worked for a mental health company. This company provided in-home services. At the time I applied. I was pretty desperate for a job. I made myself believe that home visits would not bother me. **Deep down, I had no idea what I was getting myself into.** My job position was a targeted case manager. I was in charge of providing people dealing with mental health challenges; resources. At that time, nothing was off-limits. I spent several hours alongside clients with multiple diagnoses. **To be honest, there were times when my own mental health would backfire at the peak of stressful situations.** I noticed when circumstances got out of control. Consequently, it was always around the time my prayer life was failing. **Transparently, your relationship with God must be consistent to yield results**. At times, I thought things were under control, in all reality, I was being controlled by the circumstances. My circumstances and God forced me to stay at that job to learn valuable lessons. **Obedience is key, even when it hurts.**

One of my very favorite clients, let's call her Miss Lilly. Miss Lilly, was a Caribbean goddess. She had the perfect tone of cocoa butter skin and black shoulder length shiny hair. **It's evident, this woman was always that girl**. When I first met her, **we talked for two hours about life and God.** However, **I noticed a terrible headache forming on the left side of my head**. There was something very familiar about this head pain, which I ignored. **During our conversation, we discussed deep secrets.** We also chatted about her touring in different states and chasing musical dreams. When there were a few seconds of silence, I tried to figure out how such a beautiful and talented woman's dreams could slip away. What a common story. While I listened attentively, there were awkward intermissions. Ms. Lilly would forget her thoughts and bang her hand on her head. **I knew it was time to leave when I began to feel heavy.** This feeling was also familiar. It was felt on several occasions when I was in spaces I didn't belong. Still, I stayed a little longer getting to know my client and her needs that I would assist with. After Miss Lily's husband died, her world came crashing down. She was left to fight with depression, anxiety and memory loss alone.

After I gathered my information and departed, **I realized how dizzy I was feeling**. Also, there was a sense of confusion that came over me. It was as if there was something moving around inside my head. I was very alarmed, instead of jumping to conclusions. I blamed it on skipping lunch. **Later, at night, I still felt uneasy. I dropped to my knees and prayed asking God to take away the headache that was paining me.** A few moments later, after a few burps and yawns my head began to feel normal again. What was moving around inside had calmed down a bit. **I couldn't explain it, but I was relieved**. What happened that day at Miss Lily's house continued happening around certain people I visited and came into close proximity with. **The same symptoms began to show up when I entered different environments.** It was strange, but I know God was taking me through this personal journey for a reason. **It wasn't to point out a specific population of people, it was to identify certain challenges that I was dealing with within myself.** When I thought back, I felt similar around some of my loved ones. What was God revealing? It made me question could Mental diagnosis be interchangeable? Or was it spirits taken on the role and characteristics of the diagnosis. Again, am I a Doctor or mental health expert? No. Revelation has been revealed to me though. **There is a correlation with diseases and spirits.** Think I'm fabricating? **ASK GOD.** I am just a woman with hands-on experiences and answers from the father.

My observations became more intense, God placed me in the midst of what had become my secret identity. **The longer I stayed at the company the harder I prayed**. When I went home at night, my routine was to shower, cook, **pray for the heaviness on my**

mind and my coworkers as well. Before the job, I noticed things were improving for me, clarity was finally my portion. After the job I became unstable. The environment wasn't conducive to my wellbeing. I'll never forget, laying down calling out every symptom I was feeling concerning my mental state. **After calling out names and characteristics**, I started to feel lighter and more like myself again. This went on, every day. Until I left the job. We have to pay close attention to our bodies. **Most of us are just a prayer away from freedom.**

Say What??

I'm concluding this chapter on a bright note. **Sister. If you're reading this it's not too late.** It's only the beginning. Yes, you've been called many names, jaded, left for dead, used for your body, friendships and spiritual gifts. Guess what though. You're still chosen! The heartache, confusion, abandonment and sabotage you've been through has watered your soil for greatness. **Apologize to yourself and move forward.** Once God gives us revelation of who we are there is no turning back. Who I thought I was and identified with is no longer my crutch. I'm his, and that's on PERIOD. **When those symptoms try to creep back in, I have God's word to combat them.** No shade to anyone, God is love. Without love we can not be disciples of Christ. My testimony will help unmuzzle the mouths of many. I wasn't punished, I was being prepared to equip others.

In Matthew 9:20–22, Mark 5:25–34, Luke 8:43–48 We are introduced to a woman who had been bleeding for 12 years and touched the hem of Jesus' garment. As you can imagine she was ridiculed and viewed as unclean. How dare she even have the audacity to touch someone so pure and holy? She believed that she would be healed, and because of her faith she was. Immediately, her bleeding stopped, and Jesus told her, **"Daughter, your faith has made you well. Go in peace."**

I'm not concerned, what your father, brother or granny struggled with. **You must have the faith that THING will not take you out or disturb God's mission**. We are not victims, we have victory. Daughter of God, there are millions, suffering with what you have recovered from. BE BRAVE, YOUR WORDS HAVE POWER. **This Triumph is for all of US.**

Let us Pray. A prayer for myself and my sisters!

Father God, in the mighty name of Jesus, I come before You today standing on the promises of Your Word. I break every generational curse and uproot every satanic plan sent to derail my destiny. By the blood of Jesus, I cancel every lie spoken over my life and declare that I am who You say I am — chosen, redeemed, and set apart. Holy Spirit, restore my true identity, renew my mind, and reignite my faith. Empower me to walk boldly in purpose, to speak with authority, and to live a life that testifies of Your glory. I decree and declare: no weapon formed against me and my sisters shall prosper. I am more than a conqueror through Christ Jesus, and my story will bring healing, hope, and victory. In Jesus' name, Amen."

Love you Sis, Keep the faith!

Tonekia XO